debbie bliss
BABY STYLE

debbie bliss
BABY STYLE

Irresistible Knitwear Designs and
Home Accessories for 0-3 year olds

EBURY PRESS
LONDON

This book is dedicated to the memory of my
father, William Stanley Hudson

First published in Great Britain in 2000

1 3 5 7 9 10 8 6 4 2

Text © Debbie Bliss 2000
Photographs © Sandra Lane 2000
Debbie Bliss has asserted her right to be identified as the author of this
work under the Copyright, Designs and Patents Act 1988.

First published by
Ebury Press
Random House, 20 Vauxhall Bridge Road, London SW1V 2SA

Random House Australia (Pty) Limited
20 Alfred Street, Milsons Point, Sydney, New South Wales 2061,
Australia

Random House New Zealand Limited
18 Poland Road, Glenfield, Auckland 10, New Zealand

Random House South Africa (Pty) Limited
Endulini, 5A Jubilee Road, Parktown 2193, South Africa

The Random House Group Limited Reg. No. 954009

www.randomhouse.co.uk

A CIP catalogue record for this book is available from the British Library.

Editor: Emma Callery
Designer: Christine Wood
Photographer: Sandra Lane
Stylist: Sammi Bell

ISBN 009 187082 8

Papers used by Ebury Press are natural, recyclable products made from
wood grown in sustainable forests.

Printed and bound in Singapore by Tien Wah Press

CONTENTS

Introduction

Baby Style is my latest collection of designs for babies and toddlers, a range which is now extended to include accessories and home ideas. With the renewed enthusiasm for knitting in mind, I have enjoyed the opportunity to show just how versatile the craft is, and how extensive its application. In addition to clothes, the accessory patterns here vary from a cow hide cushion to a practical denim throw and hot-water bottle cover. The collection also includes a variety of styles from a little girl's soft alpaca bolero, ideal for those more dressed-up days, to a practical hooded top and a cabled dressing gown and slippers. The 30 patterns are designed to cover a range of skills from the basic to the more experienced and I hope that within them there will be something for everyone to enjoy.

Debbie Bliss

Basic Information

NOTES

Figures for larger sizes are given in round ( ) brackets. Where only one figure appears, this applies to all sizes. Work figures given in square [ ] brackets the number of times stated afterwards. Where 0 appears, no stitches or rows are worked for this size.

The yarn amounts given in the instructions are based on average requirements and should therefore be considered approximate.

TENSION

Each pattern in this book specifies a tension – the number of stitches and rows per centimetre/inch that should be obtained with the given needles, yarn and stitch pattern. Check your tension carefully before commencing work.

Use the same yarn, needles and stitch pattern as those to be used for the main work and knit a sample at least 12.5cm/5in square. Smooth out the finished sample on a flat surface, but do not stretch it. To check the tension, place a ruler horizontally on the sample and mark 10cm/4in across with pins. Count the number of stitches between the pins. To check the row tension, place a ruler vertically on the sample and mark 10cm/4in with pins. Count the number of rows between the pins. If the number of stitches and rows is greater than specified, try again using larger needles; if less, use smaller needles. The stitch tension is the most important element to get right.

IMPORTANT

Check on the ball band for washing instructions. After washing, pat garments into shape and dry flat, away from direct heat.

Rowan Denim will shrink and fade when it is washed, just like a pair of jeans. Unlike many 'denim look' yarns, this one uses real indigo dye, which only coats the surface of the yarn, leaving a white core that is gradually exposed through washing and wearing.

When washed for the first time, the yarn will shrink by up to one-fifth in length; the width, however, will remain the same. All the necessary adjustments have been made in the instructions for the patterns specially designed for Denim.

The knitted pieces should be washed separately at a temperature of 60-70ºC (140-158ºF) before you sew the garment together. The pieces can then be tumble-dried. Dye loss will be greatest during the initial wash; the appearance of the garment will, however, be greatly enhanced with additional washing and wearing. The cream denim yarn will shrink in the same way but will not fade.

KNITTING TERMS

A few specific knitting or crochet terms may be unfamiliar to some readers. The list below explains the abbreviations used in this book to help the reader understand how to follow the various stitches and stages.

Standard abbreviations

alt = alternate

beg = begin(ning)

cont = continue

dec = decreas(e)ing

foll(s) = follow(s)ing

gst = garter stitch

inc = increas(e)ing by working into front and back of stitch

k = knit

kwise = knitwise

m1 = make one by picking up the loop lying between st just worked and next st and working into the back of it

patt = pattern

p = purl

pwise = purlwise

psso = pass slipped stitch over

rem = remaining

rep = repeat

skpo = slip 1, knit 1, pass slipped stitch over

sl = slip

st(s) = stitch(es)

st st = stocking stitch

tbl = through back of loop

tog = together

yb = yarn back

yf = yarn forward

yon = yarn over needle

yrn = yarn round needle

The following terms may be unfamiliar to US readers

UK terms	US terms
ball band	yarn wrapper
cast off	bind off
DK wool	knitting worsted yarn
double crochet stitch	single crochet stitch
make up (garment)	finish (garment)
rib	ribbing
stocking stitch	stockinette stitch
tension	gauge

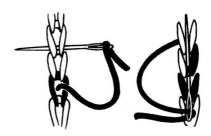

Swiss Darning
Bring needle out to front at base of stitch to be covered.
Insert needle under the base of stitch above, then back at base. Emerge at base of next stitch to be covered.

Alpaca Bolero

MATERIALS

3(4) 50g balls of Jaeger Alpaca 4 ply.
Pair each of 2¼mm (No 13/US 1) and 3mm (No 11/US 2) knitting needles.

MEASUREMENTS

To fit ages	12-18	24-36	months
Actual measurements			
Chest	60	66	cm
	23½	26	in
Length to shoulder	24	27	cm
	9½	10¾	in
Sleeve length	22	25	cm
	8¾	10	in

TENSION

28 sts and 36 rows to 10cm/4in over st st on 3mm (No 11/US 2) needles.

BACK

With 3mm (No 11/US 2) needles cast on loosely 85(93) sts.
Beg with a p row, work 39(45) rows in st st.

Shape Armholes

Cast off 5 sts at beg of next 2 rows.
Dec one st at each end of the next 5(7) rows and 4 foll alt rows. 57(61) sts.
Work straight until Back measures 12(13.5)cm/4¾(5¼)in from beg of armhole shaping, ending with a p row.

Shape Shoulders

Next row K16(17), turn and work on these sts for first side of neck shaping.
P 1 row.
Cast off.
With right side facing, rejoin yarn to rem sts, cast off centre 25(27) sts, k to end. 16(17) sts.
P 1 row.
Cast off.

LEFT FRONT

With 3mm (No 11/US 2) needles cast on loosely 20(21) sts.
Beg with a p row, cont in st st.
**Cast on loosely 2 sts at beg of the next and every foll alt row until there are 32(35) sts.
Work 3 rows straight.
Inc one st at front edge on next and every foll 4th row until there are 39(43) sts.

Shape Armhole

Next row Cast off 5 sts, k to end.

P 1 row.
Next row Work 2tog, k to end.
Next row Inc in first st, p to last 2 sts, work 2tog.
Dec one st at armhole edge on next 3(5) rows and 4 foll alt rows. 26(28) sts.
Work 2 rows.
Dec one st at neck edge on next 3 rows, then every foll alt row until 16(17) sts rem.
Work straight until Front matches Back to shoulder shaping, ending at armhole edge.
Cast off.

RIGHT FRONT

With 3mm (No 11/US 2) needles cast on loosely 20(21) sts.
P 1 row.
Complete to match Left Front from ** to end, thus reversing shaping.

SLEEVES

With 2¼mm (No 13/US 1) needles cast on 43(47) sts.
Rib row 1 K1, *p1, k1; rep from * to end.
Rib row 2 P1, *k1, p1; rep from * to end.
Work 3 more rows.
Change to 3mm (No 11/US 2) needles.
Work in st st, inc one st at each end of the 3rd and every foll 4th row until there are 67(71) sts.

Cont straight until Sleeve measures 22(25)cm/8¾(10)in from cast-on edge, ending with a wrong side row.

Shape Top

Work a further 4 rows.

Dec one st at each end of every row until 11 sts rem.

Cast off.

BACK BORDER

With 2¼mm (No 13/US 1) needles cast on 5 sts.

Cont in gst until border, when slightly stretched, fits along lower edge of Back.

Cast off.

LEFT FRONT BORDER

Join shoulder seams.

With 2¼mm (No 13/US 1) needles cast on 5 sts.

Cont in gst until border, when slightly stretched, fits along lower edge of Front, round front edge to beg of neck shaping.

Inc one st at inside edge of next and every foll 4th row until there are 15 sts.

Cont straight until shaped edge fits along shaped edge of bolero to shoulder, ending at straight edge.

Shape Collar

Next 2 rows K9, turn, sl 1, k to end.

K 6 rows.

Rep the last 8 rows until the shorter edge fits halfway across Back neck sts. Cast off.

RIGHT FRONT BORDER

Work to match Left Front border.

TO MAKE UP

Join back seam of Collar. Sew borders in place. Sew on Sleeves, sewing last 4 rows to cast-off sts at underarm. Join side and Sleeve seams.

Four-colour Cardigan

MATERIALS

2(3:3) 50g balls of Rowan Wool Cotton in Lilac (A), 1(1:2) 50g balls in Blue (B), One ball each in Cream (C) and Plum (D).
Pair each of 4mm (No 8/US 6) and 3¾mm (No 9/US 5) knitting needles.
4 buttons.

MEASUREMENTS

To fit ages	9-12	12-18	24-36 months	
Actual measurements				
Chest	60	67	75	cm
	23½	26½	29½	in
Length to shoulder	27	30	33	cm
	10½	11¾	13	in
Sleeve length	16	20	25	cm
	6¼	7¾	10	in

TENSION

22 sts and 30 rows to 10cm/4in over st st on 4mm (No 8/US 6) needles.

BACK

With 3¾mm (No 9/US 5) needles and A, cast on 66(74:82) sts.
Row 1 K2, *p2, k2; rep from * to end.
Row 2 P2, *k2, p2; rep from * to end.
Rep the last 2 rows 2(3:4) times more.
Change to 4mm (No 8/US 6) needles.
Beg with a k row, cont in st st until Back measures 27(30:33)cm/10½(11¾:13)in from cast-on edge, ending with a p row.

Shape Shoulders

Cast off 9(10:11) sts at beg of next 4 rows.
Leave rem 30(34:38) sts on a holder.

POCKET LININGS (make 2)

With 4mm (No 8/US 6) needles and A, cast on 18(18:22) sts.
Beg with a k row, work 21(25:29) rows in st st.
Leave these sts on a holder.

LEFT FRONT

With 3¾mm (No 9/US 5) needles and A, cast on 31(35:39) sts.
Row 1 K2, *p2, k2; rep from * to last 5 sts, p2, k3.
Row 2 P3, *k2, p2; rep from * to end.
Rep the last 2 rows 2(3:4) times more.
Change to 4mm (No 8/US 6) needles.
Beg with a k row, work 20(24:28) rows in st st.

Pocket Opening

Row 1 K7(10:9), the k next 18(20:22) sts and place these sts on a holder, k to end.
Row 2 P6(7:8), p across sts of pocket lining, p7(10:9).

Cont in st st until Front measures 17(18:19)cm/6½(7:7½)in from cast-on edge, ending with a p row.

Shape Neck

Next row K to last 4 sts, k2tog, k2.
Next row P to end.
Rep the last 2 rows until 18(20:22) sts rem.
Work straight until Front measures same as Back to shoulder, ending at side edge.

Shape Shoulder

Cast off 9(10:11) sts at beg of next row.
Work 1 row. Cast off rem 9(10:11) sts.

RIGHT FRONT

With 3¾mm (No 9/US 5) needles and A, cast on 31(35:39) sts.
Row 1 K3, *p2, k2; rep from * to end.
Row 2 P2, *k2, p2; rep from * to last 5 sts, k2, p3.
Rep the last 2 rows 2(3:4) times more.
Change to 4mm (No 8/US 6) needles.
Beg with a k row, work 20(24:28) rows in st st.

Pocket Opening

Row 1 K6(7:8), then k next 18(18:22) sts and place these sts on a holder, k to end.
Row 2 P7(10:9), p across sts of pocket lining, p6(7:8).
Cont in st st until Front measures 17(18:19)cm/6½(7:7½)in from cast-on edge, ending with a p row.

Shape Neck

Next row K2, skpo, k to end.
Next row P to end.
Rep the last 2 rows until 18(20:22) sts rem.

Work straight until Front measures same as Back to shoulder, ending at side edge.

Shape Shoulder

Cast off 9(10:11) sts at beg of next row.

Work 1 row. Cast off rem 9(10:11) sts.

SLEEVES

With 3¾mm (No 9/US 5) needles and C, cast on 38(42:46) sts.

Row 1 K2, *p2, k2; rep from * to end.

Row 2 P2, *k2, p2; rep from * to end.

Rep the last 2 rows 2(3:4) times more.

Change to 4mm (No 8/US 6) needles and B.

Work in st st, inc one st at each end of the 3rd and every foll 4th row until there are 58(64:70) sts.

Cont straight until Sleeve measures 16(20:25)cm/6¼(7¾:10)in from cast-on edge, ending with a wrong side row.

Cast off.

POCKET TOPS

With 3¾mm (No 9/US 5) needles, right side facing and C, k across sts from Pocket front.

Beg with row 2, work 2 rows rib as given for Back welt.

Cast off in rib.

FRONTBAND

Join shoulder seams.

With 3¾mm (No 9/US 5) needles, right side facing and D, pick up and k34(40:46) sts evenly along Right Front to beg of neck shaping, 28(30:32) sts to right shoulder, k30(34:38) sts from Back neck holder, pick up and k28(30:32) sts to beg of neck shaping, 34(40:46) sts to cast-on edge. 154(174:194) sts.

Beg with row 2, work 3 rows rib as given for Back welt.

Buttonhole row Rib 2 sts, [yrn, k2tog, rib a further 8(10:12) sts] 3 times, yrn, k2tog, rib to end.

Rib 3 rows.

Cast off in rib.

TO MAKE UP

Sew on Sleeves. Join side and Sleeve seams. Sew on buttons. Sew down Pockets and Pocket Tops.

Striped Coathanger

MATERIALS

One 50g ball each of Rowan Cotton 4 ply in Blue (A), Green (B), Plum (C), Cerise (D), Beige (E), Light Blue (F) and White (G).

Pair of 2¾mm (No 12/US 2) knitting needles.

Small amount of wadding to cover coathanger.

MEASUREMENTS

To fit a child's coathanger, 30cm/12in long.

TENSION

25 sts and 50 rows to 10cm/4in over gst on 2¾mm (No 12/US 2) needles.

TO MAKE

With 2¾mm (No 12/US 2) needles and A, cast on 20 sts.

K 3 rows.

Cont in stripe patt.

*K 2 rows B, 2 rows C, 2 rows D, 4 rows E, 6 rows F, 2 rows G, 4 rows B, 4 rows C, 2 rows D, 2 rows E, 6 rows A; rep from * until work measures 31cm/12¼in from cast-on edge.

Cast off.

TO MAKE UP

Cut wadding into 4cm/1½in wide strips, wrap round coathanger to cover, and stitch in place. With right sides together, fold knitted strip in half lengthways. Using a back stitch join both short ends, turn to right side. With folded edge uppermost, place over hook, slip over rest of hanger, and sew open edge together along under side of coathanger.

Dressing Gown with Hat and Slippers

MATERIALS
Dressing Gown: 8(10) 50g balls of Jaeger Baby Merino DK in Main Colour (M). One 50g ball in Contrast Colour (C).
Pair each of 3¼mm (No 10/US 3) and 4mm (No 8/US 6) knitting needles.
One long circular 3¼mm (No 10/US 3) knitting needle.
Cable needle.
Hat and Slippers: Two 50g balls of Jaeger Baby Merino DK in Main Colour (M). One 50g ball in Contrast Colour (C).
Pair each of 3¼mm (No 10/US 3) and 4mm (No 8/US 6) knitting needles.

MEASUREMENTS

Dressing Gown

To fit ages	1-2	2-3	years
Actual measurements			
Chest	71	86	cm
	28	33¾	in
Length to shoulder	43	53	cm
	17	20¾	in
Sleeve length	18	22	cm
with cuff turned back	7	8¾	in

Hat and Slippers

To fit ages	1-2	2-3	years

TENSION
32 sts and 30 rows to 10cm/4in over patt on 4mm (No 8/US 6) needles.
22 sts and 30 rows to 10cm/4in over st st on 4mm (No 8/US 6) needles.

ABBREVIATIONS
C6F - cable 6 front, slip next 2 sts onto cable needle and hold at of work, k2, p2, then k2 from cable needle.

Dressing Gown
BACK
With 4mm (No 8/US 6) needles and C, cast on 114(138) sts.
Row 1 P2, *k2, p2; rep from * to end.
Cut off C.
Join on M.
Cont in patt as folls:
Row 2(wrong side) K2, *p2, k2; rep from * to end.
Row 3 P2, *k2, p2; rep from * to end.
Row 4 K2, *p2, k2; rep from * to end.
Rows 5 and 6 As rows 3 and 4.

Row 7 P2, k2, p2, *C6F, p2, k2, p2; rep from * to end.
Rows 8 to 13 Rep rows 2 and 3 three times.
Rows 2 to 13 form the patt.
Cont in patt until Back measures 43(53)cm/17(20¾)in from cast-on edge, ending with a wrong side row.
Shape Shoulders
Cast off 14(17) sts at beg of next 6 rows.
Leave rem 30(36) sts on a spare needle.

POCKET LININGS (make 2)
With 4mm (No 8/US 6) needles and M, cast on 22(26) sts.
Row 1 P2, *k2, p2; rep from * to end.
Row 2 K2, *p2, k2; rep from * to end.
Rep the last 2 rows 10 times more.
Leave sts on a holder.

LEFT FRONT
With 4mm (No 8/US 6) needles and C, cast on 54(66) sts.
Row 1 P2, *k2, p2; rep from * to end.
Cut off C.
Join on M.
Cont in patt as folls:
Row 2 (wrong side) K2, *p2, k2; rep from * to end.
Row 3 P2, *k2, p2; rep from * to end.
Row 4 K2, *p2, k2; rep from * to end.
Rows 5 and 6 As rows 3 and 4.
Row 7 P2, k2, p2, *C6F, p2, k2, p2; rep from * to end.
Rows 8 to 13 Rep rows 2 and 3 three times.
Rows 2 to 13 form the patt.
Cont in patt until Front measures 22(26)cm/8½(10¼)in from cast-on edge, ending with a wrong side row.
Place Pocket
Next row Patt 18(22) sts, slip next 22(26) sts onto a holder, patt across 22(26) sts of pocket lining, patt 14(18) sts.
Cont in patt until Front measures 28(35)cm/11(13¾)in from cast-on edge, ending with a wrong side row.
Shape Neck
Next row Patt to last 5 sts, k2tog, k1, p2.
Work 2 rows in patt.
Next row K2, p1, p2tog, patt to end.
Work 2 rows in patt.
Cont in this way dec one st on every 3rd row until 42(51) sts rem.
Work straight until Front matches the same as Back to shoulder, ending at side edge.
Shape Shoulder
Cast off 14(17) sts at beg of next and foll alt row.
Work 1 row.
Cast off rem 14(17) sts.

RIGHT FRONT
With 4mm (No 8/US 6) needles and C, cast on 54(66) sts.
Row 1 P2, *k2, p2; rep from * to end.

Cut off C.

Join on M.

Cont in patt as folls:

Row 2 (wrong side) K2, *p2, k2; rep from * to end.

Row 3 P2, *k2, p2; rep from * to end.

Row 4 K2, *p2, k2; rep from * to end.

Rows 5 and 6 As rows 3 and 4.

Row 7 P2, k2, p2, *C6F, p2, k2, p2; rep from * to end.

Rows 8 to 13 Rep rows 2 and 3 three times.

Rows 2 to 13 form the patt.

Cont in patt until Front measures 22(26)cm/8½(10¼)in from cast-on edge, ending with a wrong side row.

Place Pocket

Next row Patt 14(18) sts, slip next 22(26) sts onto a holder, patt across 22(26) sts of pocket lining, patt 18(22) sts.

Cont in patt until Front measures 28(35)cm/11(13¾)in from cast-on edge, ending with a wrong side row.

Shape Neck

Next row P2, k1, skpo, patt to end.

Work 2 rows in patt.

Next row Patt to last 5 sts, p2tog tbl, p1, k2.

Work 2 rows in patt.

Cont in this way dec one st on every 3rd row until 42(51) sts rem. Work straight until Front matches the same as Back to shoulder, ending at side edge.

Shape Shoulder

Cast off 14(17) sts at beg of next and foll alt row.

Work 1 row.

Cast off rem 14(17) sts.

POCKET TOPS

With 3¼mm (No 10/US 3) needles, right side facing and C, work 2 rows in rib as set across Pocket Top.

Cast off in rib.

SLEEVES

With 4mm (No 8/US 6) needles and C, cast on 42(54) sts.

Row 1 K2, *p2, k2; rep from * to end.

Cut off C.

Join on M.

Cont for cuff as folls:

Row 2 (wrong side) P2, *k2, p2; rep from * to end.

Row 3 K2, *p2, k2; rep from * to end.

Rep the last 2 rows 6 times more and row 2 again.

Cont in patt as folls:

Row 1 P2, *k2, p2; rep from * to end.

Row 2 K2, *p2, k2; rep from * to end.

Rows 3 to 6 Rep rows 1 and 2 twice more.

Row 7 P2, k2, p2, *C6F, p2, k2, p2; rep from * to end.

Row 8 K2, *p2, k2; rep from * to end.

Rows 9 to 12 Rep rows 1 and 2 twice more.

Rows 1 to 12 form the patt.

Cont in patt, inc one st at each end of the 1st(5th) and every foll alt row until there are 76(94) sts.

Cont straight until Sleeve measures 22(26)cm/8¾(10¼)in from cast-on edge, ending with a wrong side row.

Cast off.

FRONTBAND AND COLLAR

Join shoulder seams.

With 3¼mm (No 10/US 3) circular needle, right side facing and M, starting at first row in M, pick up and k84(102) sts evenly along Right Front to beg of neck shaping, 46(49) sts to right shoulder, work in rib as set across Back neck sts, pick up and k46(49) sts to beg of neck shaping, 84(102) sts to last row in M. 290(338) sts.

Beg with row 2, work 1 row rib as given for Back.

Shape Collar

Row 1 Rib 166(193) sts, turn.

Row 2 Rib 42(48) sts, turn.

Row 3 Rib 48(54) sts, turn.

Row 4 Rib 54(60) sts, turn.

Cont in this way for a further 10 turning rows, taking an extra 6 sts, as before, on each row.

Next row Rib to end.

Rib 13 rows across all sts.

Cut off M.

With C and right side facing, pick up and k12 sts along row ends of frontband, work in rib to end of row, pick up and k12 sts along row ends of front band.

Cast off in rib.

BELT

With 3¼mm (No 10/US 3) needles and M, cast on 14 sts.

Row 1 K2, *p2, k2; rep from * to end.

Row 2 K1, p1, k2, *p2, k2; rep from * to last 2 sts, p1, k1.

Rep the last 2 rows until Belt measures 120cm/47cm from cast-on edge, ending row 2.

Cast off in rib.

TO MAKE UP

Sew on Sleeves. Join side and Sleeve seams, reversing seam on cuff. Sew down Pocket Linings and Pocket Tops. Make a Belt carrier at waist level on each side seam.

Hat

With 4mm (No 8/US 6) needles and C, cast on 98(110) sts.
Row 1 K2, *p2, k2; rep from * to end.
Cut off C.
Join on M.
Cont in patt as folls:
Row 2 P2, *k2, p2; rep from * to end.
Row 3 K2, *p2, k2; rep from * to end.
Rep the last 2 rows 3 times more and row 2 again.
Change to 3¼mm (No 10/US 3) needles, work a further 8 rows in rib, dec 2 sts on last row. 96(108) sts.
Change to 4mm (No 8/US 6) needles.
Beg with a k row, cont in st st until work measures 12(14)cm/ 4¾(5½)in from cast-on edge, ending with a wrong side row.

Shape Top

Dec row [K22(25), k2tog tbl, k2tog, k22(25)] twice.
Work 3 rows straight.
Dec row [K21(24), k2tog tbl, k2tog, k21(24)] twice.
Work 3 rows straight.
Dec row [K20(23), k2tog tbl, k2tog, k20(23)] twice.
Work 3 rows straight.
Cont in this way decreasing 4 sts on the next and every foll 4th row until 52 sts rem, then on every foll alt row until 16 sts rem.
P 1 row.
Break off yarn, thread end through rem sts, pull up and secure.
Join seam, reversing it on last 4cm/1½in of rib.
With C, make a large pompon and attach to top.

Slippers

With 3¼mm (No 10/US 3) needles and M, cast on 22(26) sts.
Work in gst throughout.
Inc one st at each end of every foll alt row until there are 38(44) sts.
Dec one st at each end of next and every foll alt row until 22(26) sts rem.

Shape Heel

Next row Cast on 8(9) sts, k these 8(9) sts, then k to end. 30(35) sts.
Inc one st at end of 7(8) foll alt rows. 37(43) sts.
K 1 row.
Next row Cast off 20(22) sts, k to last st, inc in last st. 18(22) sts.
K 18(22) rows.
Next row K2tog, k to end, turn and cast on 20(22) sts. 37(43) sts.
Dec one st at beg of 7(8) foll alt rows. 30(35) sts.
K 1 row.
Cast off.

Edging

With 3¼mm (No 10/US 3) needles, right side facing and C, pick up and k40 sts round open edge of slipper.
K 1 row.
Cast off.

TO MAKE UP

Join back heel seam. Fold Slipper along row just below cast-on sts for heel and with right sides together, join seam all round easing in fullness at toes and sewing 8(9) cast-on sts for heel and last 8(9) sts of cast-off edge to sole. Turn to right side. With C, make a pompon and attach to top of Slipper.

Heart Cushion

MATERIALS

Three 50g balls of Rowan Denim.
Pair each of 3¾mm (No 9/US 5) and 4mm (No 8/US 6) knitting
needles.
5 buttons.

MEASUREMENTS

25cm x 25cm/10in x 10in.

TENSION

20 sts and 30 rows to 10cm/4in over moss st on 4mm (No 8/US 6)
needles before washing.

BACK

With 3¾mm (No 9/US 5) needles cast on 51 sts.
K 7 rows.
Change to 4mm (No 8/US 6) needles.
Work from chart as folls:
Row 1 (right side) K to end.
Row 2 K4, p to last 4 sts, k4.
Rows 3 to 8 Rep rows 1 and 2 three times more.
Row 9 K25, p1, k25.
Row 10 K4, p20, k1, p1, k1, p20, k4.
Cont in patt to row 75.
Change to 3¾mm (No 9/US 5) needles.**
K 15 rows.
Cast off.

FRONT

Work as given for Back to **.
K 3 rows.
Buttonhole row K2, [k2tog, yf, k9] 4 times, k2tog, yf, k3.
K 3 rows.
Cast off.

TO MAKE UP

See page 6 for Basic Information on making up Denim yarn.
With wrong sides together and leaving last 8 rows of Back free, join
side and and lower seam. Fold final rows of back to inside. Sew on
buttons.

The pattern for the Rabbit in Sweater included in the photograph
opposite is given in *Toy Knits*, also by Debbie Bliss.

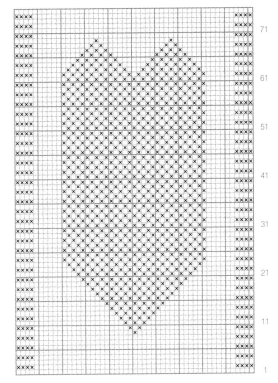

Key

☐ K on right side
  P on wrong side

✕ P on right side
  K on wrong side

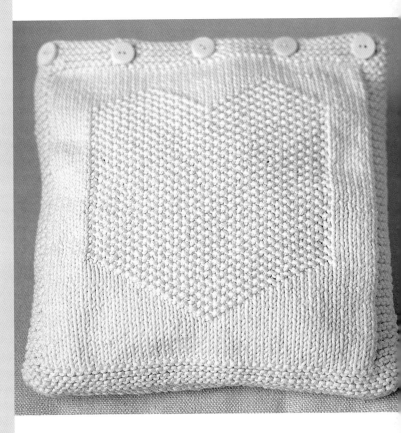

Simple Top with Picot Edging

MATERIALS
3(4) 50g balls of Jaeger Matchmaker Merino 4 ply.
Pair each of 2¾mm (No 12/US 2) and 3¼mm (No 10/US 3) needles.
2 buttons.

MEASUREMENTS

To fit ages	6-12	12-18	months
Actual measurements			
Chest	56	62	cm
	22	24½	in
Length to shoulder	30	35	cm
	12	13¾	in
Sleeve length	18	22	cm
	7	8¾	in

TENSION
28 sts and 36 rows to 10cm/4in over st st on 3¼mm (No 10/US 3) needles.

BACK
With 2¾mm (No 12/US 2) needles cast on 78(86) sts.
Rib row *K1, p1; rep from * to end.
Rep the last row for 2.5(3)cm/1(1¼)in ending with a wrong side row.
Change to 3¼mm (No 10/US 3) needles.
Cont in st st until Back measures 30(35)cm/12(13¾)in from cast-on edge, ending with a p row.
Shape Shoulders
Cast off 11(12) sts at beg of next 4 rows.
Leave rem 34(38) sts on a holder.

FRONT
Work as given for Back until Front measures 20(23)cm/8(9)in from cast-on edge, ending with a p row.
Front Opening
Next row K36(40), turn and work on these sts for first side of neck.
Work straight for 5(6)cm/2(2½)in, ending at side edge.
Shape Neck
Next row K to last 7(8) sts, leave these sts on a safety pin.
Dec one st at neck edge on every row until 22(24) sts rem.
Work straight until Front measures same as Back to shoulder, ending at side edge.
Shape Shoulder
Cast off 11(12) sts at beg of next row.
Work 1 row. Cast off rem 11(12) sts.
With right side facing, cast off centre 6 sts, work to end.
Complete to match first side.

SLEEVES
With 2¾mm (No 12/US 2) needles cast on 44(48) sts.
Work 2.5(3)cm/1(1¼)in k1, p1 rib, ending with a wrong side row.

Change to 3¼mm (No 10/US 3) needles.
Work in st st, inc one st at each end of every 3rd and every foll 4th row alternately until there are 72(80) sts.
Cont straight until Sleeve measures 18(22)cm/7(8¾)in from cast-on edge, ending with a wrong side row.
Cast off.

BUTTON BAND
With 2¾mm (No 12/US 2) needles and right side facing, pick up and k19(21) sts down left side of front neck opening.
Rib row 1 (wrong side) P1, *k1, p1; rep from * to end.
Rib row 2 K1, *p1, k1; rep from * to end.
Work a further 5 rows in rib.
Cast off.

BUTTONHOLE BAND
With 2¾mm (No 12/US 2) needles and right side facing, pick up and k 19(21) sts up right side of front neck opening.
Work 3 rows k1, p1 rib as given for Button Band.
Buttonhole row Rib 3, yf, rib 2tog, rib 9(11), rib 2tog, yf, rib 3.
Work 3 rows rib.
Cast off row Cast off kwise one st, [sl st used in casting off back onto left-hand needle, cast on 2 sts kwise, cast off 4 sts kwise] to end. Fasten off.

COLLAR
Join shoulder seams.
With 2¾mm (No 12/US 2) needles and right side facing, pick up and k3 sts from second half of Buttonhole Band, k7(8) sts from safety pin, pick up and k20(22) sts up right side of Front neck, k34(38) sts from Back neck, pick up and k21(23) sts down left side of Front neck, 7(8) sts from safety pin, k3 sts from first half of Button Band.
95(105) sts.
Cont in k1, p1, rib as given for Button Band.
Next row Rib 68(75) sts, turn.
Next row Rib 42(46) sts, turn.
Next row Rib 46(50) sts, turn.
Next row Rib 50(54) sts, turn.
Next row Rib 54(58) sts, turn.
Next row Rib 58(62) sts, turn.
Next row Rib 62(66) sts, turn.
Next row Rib 66(70) sts, turn.
Next row Rib to end.
Work 5(5.5)cm/2(2¼)in rib on these sts.
Cast off row Cast off kwise one st, [sl st used in casting off back onto left-hand needle, cast on 2 sts kwise, cast off 4 sts kwise] to end. Fasten off.

TO MAKE UP
Sew on Sleeves. Join together the side and Sleeve seams. Lap Buttonhole Band over Button Band and catch in place. Sew on buttons.

Snowflake Skirt

MATERIALS
3(4) 50g balls of Jaeger Matchmaker Merino 4 ply in Red (M).
Small amount in Contrast Colour (C).
Pair each of 2¾mm (No 12/US 2) and 3¼mm (No 10/US 3) needles.
Shirring elastic.
2 buttons.

MEASUREMENTS

To fit ages	6-12	12-18	months
Actual measurements			
length	21	25	cm
	8½	10	in

TENSION
28 sts and 36 rows to 10cm/4in over st st on 3¼mm (No 10/US 3) needles.

NOTE
Motifs are Swiss darned after completion (see diagrams on page 7).

BACK
With 2¾mm (No 12/US 2) needles and M, cast on 66(70) sts.
Rib row 1 P2, *k2, p2; rep from * to end.
Rib row 2 K2, *p2, k2; rep from * to end.
Rep the last 2 rows 4 times more, then row 1 again.
Inc row Rib 3(1), *m1, rib 3; rep from * to end. 87(93) sts.
**Change to 3¼mm (No 10/US 3) needles.
Cont in st st until Back measures 4cm/1½in from cast-on edge, ending with a p row.

Shape skirt
Inc row 1 K7(6), [m1, k9(10)] 8 times, m1, k8(7). 96(102) sts.
Work 9 rows straight.
Inc row 2 K8(7), [m1, k10(11)] 8 times, m1, k8(7). 105(111) sts.
Work 9 rows straight.
Inc row 3 K8(7), [m1, k11(12)] 8 times, m1, k9(8). 114(120) sts.
Work 9 rows straight.
Inc row 4 K9(8), [m1, k12(13)] 8 times, m1, k9(8). 123(129) sts.
Work 9 rows straight.
Inc row 5 K9(8), [m1, k13(14)] 8 times, m1, k10(9). 132(138) sts.
Work 9 rows straight.
Cont in st st until Back measures 21(25)cm/8¼(10)in from cast-on edge, ending with a k row.
Change to 2¼mm (No 12/US 2) needles.
K 4 rows,
Cast off. **

FRONT
With 2¾mm (No 12/US 2) needles and M, cast on 80(85) sts.

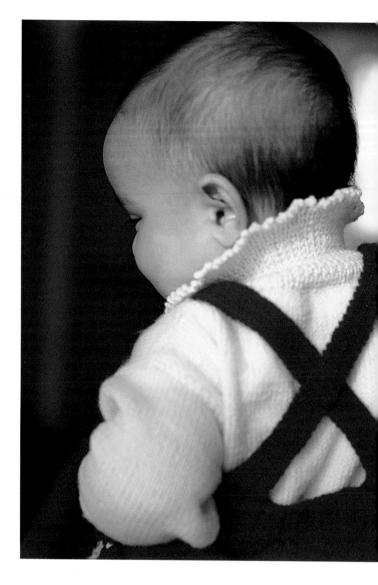

Row 1 (right side) [P2, k2] 3 times, p56(61), [k2, p2] 3 times.
Row 2 [K2, p2] 3 times, k56(61), [p2, k2] 3 times.
Row 3 [P2, k2] twice, p2, k60(65), p2, [k2, p2] twice.
Row 4 [K2, p2], k2, p60(65), k2, [p2, k2] twice.
Rows 5 and 6 As rows 1 and 2.
Row 7 (buttonhole row) [P2, k2] twice, p2, k19(20), k2tog, yf, k18(21), yf, skpo, k19(20), p2, [k2, p2] twice.
Row 8 As row 4.
Row 9 As row 1.
Inc row Rib 12, k1(2), [m1, k9(8)] 6(7) times, m1, k1(3), rib 12. 87(93) sts.
Work as given for Back from ** to **.

STRAPS (make 2)
With 2¾mm (No 12/US 2) needles and M, cast on 12 sts.
Row 1 K3, p2, k2, p2, k3.

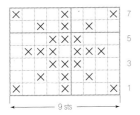

Key

☐ Main Colour

✕ Contrast Colour

Row 2 K1, [p2, k2] twice, p2, k1.
Rep the last 2 rows until Strap measures 38cm/15in from cast-on edge.
Cast off.

TO MAKE UP

Swiss Darning: With Contrast Colour and working from hem upwards, starting on the 4th row of st st, work as folls: miss 4½ sts from right-hand edge, working from chart, place first row of motif over next nine sts, then complete motif. [Miss next 10(11) sts, working from chart, place first row of motif over next nine sts, then complete motif] 6 times, leaving last 4½ sts free. Join side seams. If necessary, run 3 or 4 rows of shirring elastic through rib rows at back. Sew straps to back. Sew on buttons.

Snowflake Bootees

MATERIALS

One 50g ball of Jaeger Matchmaker Merino 4 ply in Red (M). Small amount in Contrast Colour.
Pair each of 2¾mm (No 12/US 2) and 3¼mm (No 10/US 3) knitting needles.

MEASUREMENTS

To fit ages   3-6   months.

TENSION

28 sts and 36 rows to 10cm/4in over st st on 3¼mm (No 10/US 3) needles.

NOTE

Motifs are Swiss darned after completion (see diagrams on page 7).

TO MAKE

With 2¾mm (No 12/US 2) needles and M, cast on 26 sts.
K 1 row.
Row 1 K1, yf, k11, [yf, k1] twice, yf, k11, yf, k1.
Row 2 and 3 foll alt rows K to end, working k1 tbl into yf of previous row.
Row 3 K2, yf, k11, yf, k2, yf, k3, yf, k11, yf, k2.
Row 5 K3, yf, k11, [yf, k4] twice, yf, k11, yf, k3.
Row 7 K4, yf, k11, yf, k5, yf, k6, yf, k11, yf, k4.
Row 9 K5, yf, k11, [yf, k7] twice, yf, k11, yf, k5.
Row 10 As row 2.
Change to 3¼mm (No 10/US 3) needles.
Beg with a k row, work 7 rows in st st.
Change to 2¾mm (No 12/US 2) needles.
K 3 rows.
Change to 3¼mm (No 10/US 3) needles.
Shape Instep
Row 1 K29, skpo, turn.
Row 2 Sl 1, p7, p2tog, turn.
Row 3 Sl 1, k7, skpo, turn.
Rows 4 to 14 Rep rows 1 and 2 five times more, then row 1 again.
Row 15 Sl 1, k7, skpo, k to end.
Row 16 P21, p2tog, p to end. 35 sts.

K 1 row.
P 1 row.
Next row K1, *p1, k1; rep from * to end.
Next row P1, *k1, p1; rep from * to end.
Rep the last 2 rows 3 times more, then the first of these rows again.
Next row Rib 17, cast off one st, rib to end.
Working on last set of 17 sts, rib 11 rows.
Break off yarn.
With 2¾mm (No 12/US 2) needles and right side of cuff facing, pick up and k8 sts along row ends of cuff, then rib sts on needle.
Cast off row Cast off kwise one st, [sl st used in casting off back onto left-hand needle, cast on 2 sts kwise, cast off 4 sts kwise] to end. Fasten off.
Rejoin yarn at centre to rem 17 sts and rib 11 rows.
Change to 2¾mm (No 12/US 2) needles.
Next row Rib to end, then pick up and k8 sts along row ends of cuff.
Cast off row Cast off kwise one st, [sl st used in casting off back onto left-hand needle, cast on 2 sts kwise, cast off 4 sts kwise] to end. Fasten off.

TO MAKE UP

Swiss darn motif on instep with Contrast Colour. Join sole and back seam, reversing seam for cuff. Turn back cuff.

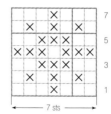

Key
☐ Main Colour
✕ Contrast Colour

Cow Cushion

MATERIALS

Two 50g balls each of Jaeger Matchmaker DK in Cream (C) and Black (B).
Pair of 3¾mm (No 9/US 5) knitting needles.
4 buttons.
30cm x 30cm/12in x 12in cushion pad.

MEASUREMENTS

Cushion cover measures 30cm x 30cm/12in x 12in.

TENSION

24 sts and 46 rows to 10cm/4in over gst on 3¾mm (No 9/US 5) needles.

NOTE

Read chart from right to left on right side rows and from left to right on wrong side rows.
Each square on chart represents one stitch and **2 rows**.
Use separate balls of yarn for each area of colour and twist yarns on wrong side when changing colour to avoid holes.

BACK

With 3¾mm (No 9/US 5) needles and C, cast on 74 sts.
K 5 rows.
Work in patt from chart 1 as folls:
Row 1 (right side) K4C, k across row 1 of chart 1, k30C.
Row 2 K30C, k across row 2 of chart 1, k4C.
These 2 rows set the patt from chart 1.
Patt a further 74 rows.
K 4 rows in C.
Work in patt from chart 2 as folls:
Row 1 (right side) K33C, k across row 1 of chart 2, k3C.
Row 2 K3C, k across row 2 of chart 2, k33C.
These 2 rows set the patt from chart 2.
Patt a further 52 rows.
Cont in C only.
K 2 rows.
Mark each end of last row.
K 19 rows.
Cast off.

FRONT

With 3¾mm (No 9/US 5) needles and C, cast on 74 sts.
K 5 rows.
Work in patt from chart 1 as folls:
Row 1 (right side) K4C, k across row 1 of chart 1, k30C.
Row 2 K30C, k across row 2 of chart 1, k4C.
These 2 rows set the patt from chart 1.
Patt a further 74 rows.
K 4 rows in C.

Work in patt from chart 2 as folls:
Row 1 (right side) K33C, k across row 1 of chart 2, k3C.
Row 2 K3C, k across row 2 of chart 2, k33C.
These 2 rows set the patt from chart 2.
Patt a further 46 rows.
Buttonhole row 1 Patt 10, [cast off 3 sts, patt a further 13 sts] 3 times, cast off 3, patt to end.
Buttonhole row 2 Patt to end, casting on 3 sts over those cast off in previous row.
Patt a further 4 rows.
Cont in C only.
K 3 rows.
Cast off.

TO MAKE UP

Turn the 19 rows on Back, above markers, to wrong side and catch at sides. Place cast-off edge of Front along folded edge of Back and join lower and 2 side seams. Sew on buttons.

Chart 1

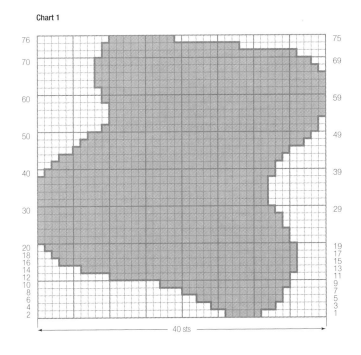

40 sts

Chart 2

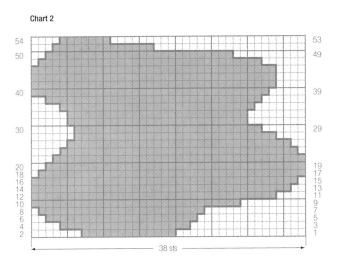

38 sts

Key

☐ With C, one st and **2 rows**

▨ With B, one st and **2 rows**

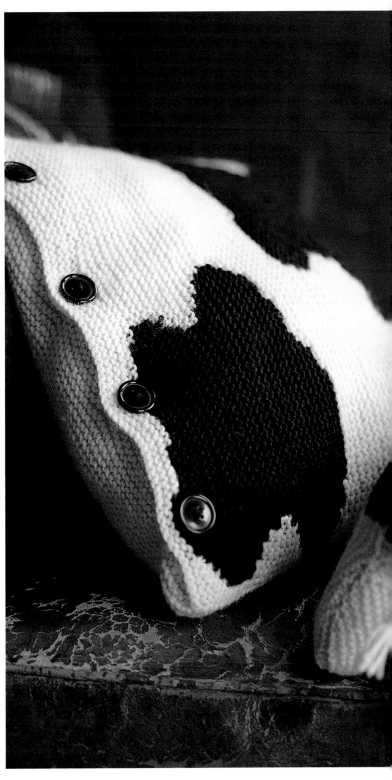

Frilled Edge Crossover Jacket

MATERIALS
3(4:4) 50g balls of Rowan Felted Tweed DK.
Pair each of 3¾mm (No 9/US 5) and 4mm (No 8/US 6) knitting needles.
One 4mm (No 8/US 6) circular knitting needle.

MEASUREMENTS

To fit ages	1	2	3 years	
Actual measurements				
Chest	56	62	70	cm
	22	24½	27½	in
Length to shoulder	32	38	45	cm
	12½	15	17¾	in
Sleeve length	18	22	24	cm
	7	8½	9½	in

TENSION
22 sts and 32 rows to 10cm/4in over st st on 4mm (No 8/US 6) needles.

BACK
With 3¾mm (No 9/US 5) needles cast on 61(69:77) sts.
Rib row 1 P1, *k1, p1; rep from * to end.
Rib row 2 K1, *p1, k1; rep from * to end.
Rep the last 2 rows 3 times more.
Change to 4mm (No 8/US 6) needles.
Beg with a k row, work 96(116:138) rows in st st.
Shape Shoulders
Cast off 8(9:10) sts at beg of next 4 rows.
Cast off rem 29(33:37) sts.

RIGHT FRONT
With 3¾mm (No 9/US 5) needles cast on 55(63:71) sts.
Rib row 1 K1, *p1, k1; rep from * to end.
Rib row 2 P1, *k1, p1; rep from * to end.
Rep the last 2 rows 3 times more.
Change to 4mm (No 8/US 6) needles.
Beg with a k row, work 46(56:66) rows in st st.
Shape Neck
Row 1 K1, skpo, k to end.
Row 2 P to last 3 sts, p2tog tbl, p1.
Cont in this way, dec on every row until 16(18:20) sts rem.
Work 12(16:22) rows straight.
Shape Shoulder
Cast off 8(9:10) sts at beg of next row.
Work 1 row.
Cast off rem 8(9:10) sts.

LEFT FRONT
With 3¾mm (No 9/US 5) needles cast on 55(63:71) sts.

Rib row 1 K1, *p1, k1; rep from * to end.
Rib row 2 P1, *k1, p1; rep from * to end.
Rep the last 2 rows 3 times more.
Change to 4mm (No 8/US 6) needles.
Beg with a k row, work 46(56:66) rows in st st.
Shape Neck
Row 1 K to last 3 sts, k2tog, k1.
Row 2 P1, p2tog, p to end.
Cont in this way, dec on every row until 16(18:20) sts rem.
Work 11(15:21) rows straight.
Shape Shoulder
Cast off 8(9:10) sts at beg of next row.
Work 1 row.
Cast off rem 8(9:10) sts.

SLEEVES
With 3¾mm (No 9/US 5) needles cast on 34(38:42) sts.
Rib row *K1, p1; rep from * to end.
Rep the last row 5 times more.
Change to 4mm (No 8/US 6) needles.

Work in st st, inc one st at each end of the 3rd and every foll 4th row until there are 58(66:74) sts.
Cont straight until Sleeve measures 18(22:24)cm/7(8½:9½)in from cast-on edge, ending with a wrong side row. Cast off.

SIDE EDGINGS
With 3¾mm (No 9/US 5) needles and right side facing, pick up and k39(45:51) sts evenly along short side of Right Front.
Work 6 rows in rib as given for Back, **at the same time** dec one st at top edge on every row.
Cast off in rib.
Work Left Front edging in same way.

TIES (make 2)
With 3¾mm (No 9/US 5) needles cast on 7 sts.
Rib row 1 K1, *p1, k1; rep from * to end.
Rib row 2 K2, p1, k1, p1, k2.
Rep the last 2 rows until Tie measures 36(42:48)cm/14¼(16½:19)in. Cast off.

NECK FRILL
Join shoulder seams.
With 4mm (No 8/US 6) circular knitting needle and right side facing, starting at cast-off edge of Right Front edging, pick up and k60(70:82) sts evenly along Right Front neck edge, 29(33:37) sts across Back neck and 60(70:82) sts evenly along Left Front neck edge, ending at cast-off edge of Left Front edging. 149(173:201) sts.
Work backwards and forwards in rows as folls:
Row 1 K1, *yf, k1; rep from * to end.
Row 2 P1, *k1, p1; rep from * to end.
Row 3 K1, *p1, k1; rep from * to end.
Rep the last 2 rows 2(3:3) times more.
Cast off kwise.

TO MAKE UP
Sew on Sleeves. Sew Ties to Fronts level with neck shaping. Join side and Sleeve seams, leaving small opening in right seam level with neck shaping.

Hot Water Bottle Cover with Billy Bear

MATERIALS
Hot Water Bottle Cover: Two 50g balls of Jaeger Extra Fine Merino DK in Main Colour (M). Small amount in Contrast Colour (C). Pair each of 3¼mm (No 10/US 3) and 4mm (No 8/US 6) knitting needles.
Billy Bear: One 50g ball of Jaeger Alpaca 4 ply. Oddment of brown yarn for embroidery.
Pair of 3¼mm (No 10/US 3) knitting needles.
Stuffing.

MEASUREMENTS
To fit a small hot water bottle 20cm/8in wide and 25cm/10in long (excluding neck).
Bear is approximately 15cm/6in high.

TENSION
With DK yarn, 22 sts and 30 rows to 10cm/4in over st st on 4mm (No 8/US 6) needles.
With 4 ply yarn, 28 sts and 36 rows to 10cm/4in over st st on 3¼mm (No 10/ US 3) needles.

Hot Water Bottle Cover
FRONT
With 4mm (No 8/US 6) needles and M, cast on 42 sts.
Beg with a k row, cont in st st, inc one st at each end of the 2nd, 3rd and 5th rows. 48 sts.
Work a further 65 rows straight.

Shape Top
Cast off 3 sts at beg of next 8 rows. 24 sts.
Leave these sts on a holder.

BACK
Lower Part
With 4mm (No 8/US 6) needles and M, cast on 42 sts.
Beg with a k row, cont in st st, inc one st at each end of the 2nd, 3rd and 5th rows. 48 sts.
Work a further 25 rows straight.
Mark each end of last row.
Work a further 15 rows.
Change to 3¼mm (No 10/US 3) needles.
K 2 rows.
Cast off.

Upper Part
With 3¼mm (No 10/US 3) needles and M, cast on 48 sts.
K 3 rows.
Change to 4mm (No 8/US 6) needles.
Beg with a k row, work 15 rows in st st.
Mark each end of last row.

Work a further 23 rows.
Shape Top
Cast off 3 sts at beg of next 8 rows. 24 sts.
Collar
Change to 3¼mm (No 10/US 3) needles.
Next row K11, k2tog, k11, then k11, k2tog, k11 across sts of front. 46 sts.
Rib row 1 K2, *p2, k2; rep from * to end.
Rib row 2 P2, *k2, p2; rep from * to end.
Rep these 2 rows 8 times more.
Change to 4mm (No 8/US 6) needles.
Rib a further 18 rows.
Cut off M.
Join in C.
Rib 1 row.
Cast off.

POCKET
With 4mm (No 8/US 6) needles and M, cast on 28 sts.
Rib row 1 K3, *p2, k2; rep from * to last 5 sts, p2, k3.
Rib row 2 P3, *k2, p2; rep from * to last 5 sts, k2, p3.
Rep the last 2 rows 14 times more.
Cut off M.
Join in C.
Rib 1 row.
Cast off.

TO MAKE UP
Sew Pocket on Front.
Place upper part of Back over lower part, matching cast-on edge of upper part with markers on lower part, and cast-off edge of lower part to markers on upper part. Join at sides. Join Back to Front, reversing seam on Collar.

Billy Bear

RIGHT LEG

With 3¼mm (No 10/US 3) needles cast on 10 sts.
P 1 row.
Next row K1, [m1, k1] to end.
P 1 row.
Next row K7, m1, k1, m1, k8, m1, k1, m1, k2. 23 sts.
Work 3 rows st st.
Next row K4, [skpo] twice, [k2tog] twice, k11.
Next row P9, [p2tog] twice, [p2tog tbl] twice, p2.
Next row K3, k2tog, k10. 14 sts.
**Work 11 rows, inc one st at each end of 4th row. 16 sts.
Next row K1, k2tog, k1, skpo, k3, k2tog, k1, skpo, k2.
P 1 row.
Next row [K2tog, k1, skpo, k1] twice.
Next row [P2tog] to end.
Break off yarn. Thread end through rem sts, pull up and secure.
Leaving an opening, join seams. Stuff and close opening.

LEFT LEG

With 3¼mm (No 10/US 3) needles cast on 10 sts.
P 1 row.
Next row K1, [m1, k1] to end.
P 1 row.
Next row K2, m1, k1, m1, k8, m1, k1, m1, k7. 23 sts.
Work 3 rows st st.
Next row K11, [skpo] twice, [k2tog] twice, k4.
Next row P2, [p2tog] twice, [p2tog tbl] twice, p9.
Next row K10, k2tog, k3. 14 sts.
Complete as given for Right Leg from ** to end.

BODY

Beg at neck edge.
With 3¼mm (No 10/US 3) needles cast on 15 sts.
P 1 row.
Next row K1, [m1, k1] to end. 29 sts.
Beg with a p row, work 5 rows st st.
Next row [K7, m1] twice, k1, [m1, k7] twice.
Work 3 rows st st.
Next row K16, m1, k1, m1, k16. 35 sts.
Work 5 rows st st.
Next row K15, skpo, k1, k2tog, k15.
Work 3 rows st st.
Next row K14, skpo, k1, k2tog, k14.
Work 3 rows st st.
Next row K1, [k2tog] to end. 16 sts.
P 1 row.
Cast off.

ARMS (make 2)

With 3¼mm (No 10/US 3) needles cast on 6 sts.
P 1 row.
Next row K1, [m1, k1] to end.

P 1 row.
Next row K1, [m1, k4, m1, k1] twice. 15 sts.
Work 3 rows st st.
Next row K1, [skpo, k2, k2tog, k1] twice.
Work 13 rows, inc one st at each end of 4th row. 13 sts.
Next row K1, [skpo, k1, k2tog, k1] twice.
P 1 row.
Next row K1, [k2tog] to end.
Break off yarn. Thread end through rem sts, pull up and secure.
Leaving an opening, join seams. Stuff and close opening.

HEAD

Begin at back.
With 3¼mm (No 10/US 3) needles cast on 7 sts.
P 1 row.
Next row K1, [m1, k1] to end.
Rep the last 2 rows once more. 25 sts.
Work 3 rows st st.
Next row K1, [m1, k3] to end. 33 sts.
Work 13 rows st st.
Next row K1, [k2tog] to end.
Work 3 rows st st.
Next row K1, [k2tog] to end. 9 sts.
P 1 row.
Break off yarn. Thread end through rem sts, pull up and secure.
Leaving an opening, join seams. Stuff and close opening.

EARS (make 2)

With 3¼mm (No 10/US 3) needles cast on 3 sts.
P 1 row.
Next row K1, [m1, k1] to end.
Rep the last 2 rows once more. 9 sts.
P 1 row.
Next row K1, m1, k2, m1, k3, m1, k2, m1, k1. 13 sts.
Work 5 rows st st.
Next row [K1, skpo] twice, k1. [k2tog, k1] twice.
P 1 row.
Next row [Skpo] twice, k1, [k2tog] twice.
P 1 row.
Next row Skpo, k1, k2tog.
Cast off.

TO MAKE UP

Join back seam of body, then cast-off edge. Stuff. Gather neck edge, pull up and secure. Sew head in place. Fold ears in half widthwise and stitch together open edge.
Sew ears in place. With brown yarn, embroider face features.
Attach yarn at seam 1cm/¼in below top of one arm, thread through body at shoulder position, then attach other arm, pull tightly and thread through body again in same place, attach yarn to first arm and fasten off. Attach legs at hip position in same way as arms.

Four-colour Sweater

MATERIALS
2(2:3) 50g balls of Rowan Wool Cotton in Blue (A), 1(2:2) 50g balls in Navy (B), One ball each in Cream (C) and Lime (D).
Pair each of 4mm (No 8/US 6) and 3¾mm (No 9/US 5) knitting needles.

MEASUREMENTS

To fit ages	6	9	12	months
Actual measurements				
Chest	56	60	64	cm
	22	23½	25	in
Length to shoulder	24	27	30	cm
	9½	10½	11¾	in
Sleeve length	15	17	19	cm
	6	6¾	7½	in

TENSION
22 sts and 30 rows to 10cm/4in over st st on 4mm (No 8/US 6) needles.

BACK
With 3¾mm (No 9/US 5) needles and C, cast on 62(66:70) sts.
Row 1 K2, *p2, k2; rep from * to end.
Row 2 P2, *k2, p2; rep from * to end.
Rep the last 2 rows 2(3:4) times more.
Change to 4mm (No 8/US 6) needles and A.
Beg with a k row, cont in st st until Back measures 24(27:30)cm/9½(10½:11¾)in, from cast-on edge, ending with a p row.
Shape Shoulders
Cast off 9(9:10) sts at beg of next 2 rows and 9(10:10) sts on foll 2 rows.
Leave rem 26(28:30) sts on a holder.

FRONT
Work as given for Back until Front measures 16(18:20)cm/6¼(7:7¾)in from cast-on edge, ending with a p row.
Front Opening
Next row K29(31:33), turn and work on these sts for first side of neck.
Work straight for 5cm/2in, ending at side edge.
Shape Neck
Next row K to last 4(5:6) sts, leave these sts on a safety pin.
Dec one st at neck edge on every row until 18(19:20) sts rem.
Work straight until Front measures same as Back to shoulder, ending at side edge.
Shape Shoulder
Cast off 9(9:10) sts at beg of next row.
Work 1 row. Cast off rem 9(10:10) sts.

With right side facing, rejoin A, cast off centre 4 sts, k to end.
Work straight for 5cm/2in, ending at side edge.
Shape Neck
Next row P to last 4(5:6) sts, leave these sts on a safety pin.
Dec one st at neck edge on every row until 18(19:20) sts rem.
Work straight until Front measures same as Back to shoulder, ending at side edge.

Shape Shoulder

Cast off 9(9:10) sts at beg of next row.

Work 1 row. Cast off rem 9(10:10) sts.

SLEEVES

With 3¾mm (No 9/US 5) needles and D, cast on 34(38:42) sts.

Row 1 K2, *p2, k2; rep from * to end.

Row 2 P2, *k2, p2; rep from * to end.

Rep the last 2 rows 2(3:4) times more.

Change to 4mm (No 8/US 6) needles and B.

Work in st st, inc one st at each end of the 3rd and every foll 4th row until there are 52(58:64) sts.

Cont straight until Sleeve measures 15(17:19)cm/6(6¾:7½)in from cast-on edge, ending with a wrong side row. Cast off.

LEFT FRONT BAND

With 3¾mm (No 9/US 5) needles, right side facing and D, pick up and k14 sts down left side of front neck opening.

Work 5 rows k2, p2 rib as given for Back welt.

Cast off in rib.

RIGHT FRONT BAND

With 3¾mm (No 9/US 5) needles, right side facing and B, pick up and k14 sts up right side of front neck opening.

Work 5 rows k2, p2 rib as given for Back welt.

Cast off in rib.

COLLAR

Join shoulder seams.

With 3¾mm (No 9/US 5) needles, right side facing and B, pick up and k3 sts from second half of Right Front Band, k4(5:6) sts from safety pin, pick up and k11(13:15) sts up right side of Front neck, k26(28:30) sts from Back neck, pick up and k11(13:15) sts down left side of Front neck, 4(5:6) sts from safety pin, k3 sts from first half of Left Front Band.

62(70:78) sts.

Work in rib as given on Back welt.

Next row Rib 48(53:58) sts, turn.

Next row Rib 34(36:38) sts, turn.

Next row Rib 38(40:42) sts, turn.

Next row Rib 42(44:46) sts, turn.

Next row Rib 46(48:50) sts, turn.

Next row Rib 50(52:54) sts, turn.

Next row Rib to end.

Work a further 5(5.5:6)cm/2(2¼:2½)in in rib on these sts.

Cast off.

MAKE UP

Sew on Sleeves. Join side and Sleeve seams. Lap Right Front Band over Left Front Band and catch in place.

Kimono, Pants and Bootees

MATERIALS

Kimono and Bootees: 2(2:3) 50g balls of Jaeger Alpaca 4 ply each in of Main Colour (M) and Contrast Colour (C).
Pair of 3¼mm (No 10/US 3) knitting needles.
Pants: 2(2:3) 50g balls of Jaeger Alpaca 4 ply in Main (M).
Pair of 3¼mm (No 10/US 3) knitting needles.
Length of 1.5cm/½in wide elastic for waist.

MEASUREMENTS

To fit ages	3-6	6-9	9-12	months

Kimono
Actual measurements

Chest	54	58	63	cm
	21¼	22¾	24¾	in
Length	24	27	32	cm
	9½	10½	12½	in
Sleeve length	16	18	22	cm
	6¼	7	8¾	in

Pants

Waist to crotch	22	27	32	cm
	8¾	10½	12½	in
Inside leg	7	9	11	cm
	2¾	3½	4¼	in

TENSION

25 sts and 54 rows to 10cm/4in over gst on 3¼mm (No 10/US 3) needles.

Kimono

BACK

With 3¼mm (No 10/US 3) needles and M, cast on 67(73:79)sts.

K 5 rows.

Cont in gst and stripes of 2 rows C and 2 rows M until Back measures 24(27:32)cm/9½(10½:12½)in from cast-on edge, ending with a wrong side row.

Shape Shoulders

Cast off 10(11:12) sts at beg of next 4 rows.

Cast off rem 27(29:31) sts.

LEFT FRONT

With 3¼mm (No 10/US 3) needles and M, cast on 57(61:65)sts.

K 5 rows.

Cont in gst and stripes as folls:

Row 1 (right side) With C k to last 3 sts, join on a small ball of M, with M, k3.

Row 2 With M, k3, with C, k to end.

Row 3 With M, k to end.

Row 4 With M, k to end.

Rep the last 4 rows until Front measures 7(9:11)cm/2¾(3½:4¼)in from cast-on edge, ending with row 1.

Shape Neck

Next 2 rows With M, k1, sl 1pwise, turn, yb, sl 1, k1.

Next 2 rows With M, k2, sl 1pwise, turn, yb, sl 1, k2.

Next 2 rows With M, k3, sl 1pwise, turn, yb, sl 1, k3.

Next 2 rows With M, k2, sl 1pwise, turn, yb, sl 1, k2.

Next 2 rows With M, k1, sl 1pwise, turn, yb, sl 1, k1.

Next row With M, k3, with C, k to end.

Next row With M, k to last 5 sts, k2tog, k3.

Next row With M, k to end.

Next row With C, k to last 5 sts, k2tog, with M, k3.

Next row With M, k3, with C, k to end.

Rep the last 4 rows until 20(22:24) sts rem.

Work straight until Front matches Back to shoulder shaping, ending at side edge.

Shape Shoulder

Cast off 10(11:12) sts at beg of next row.

Work 1 row. Cast off rem 10(11:12) sts.

RIGHT FRONT

With 3¼mm (No 10/US 3) needles and M, cast on 57(61:65)sts.

K 5 rows.

Cont in gst and stripes as folls:

Row 1 With small ball of M, k3, with C, k to end.

Row 2 With C, k to last 3 sts, with M, k3.

Row 3 With M, k to end.

Row 4 With M, k to end.

Rep the last 4 rows until Front measures 7(9:11)cm/2¾(3½:4¼)in from cast-on edge, ending with row 2.

Shape Neck
Next 2 rows With M, k1, sl 1pwise, turn, yb, sl 1, k1.
Next 2 rows With M, k2, sl 1pwise, turn, yb, sl 1, k2.
Next 2 rows With M, k3, sl 1pwise, turn, yb, sl 1, k3.
Next 2 rows With M, k2, sl 1pwise, turn, yb, sl 1, k2.
Next 2 rows With M, k1, sl 1pwise, turn, yb, sl 1, k1.
Next row With M, k3, skpo to end.
Next row With M, k to end.
Next row With M, k3, with C, skpo, to end.
Next row With C, k to last 3 sts, with M, k3.
Rep the last 4 rows until 20(22:24) sts rem.
Work straight until Front matches Back to shoulder shaping, ending at side edge.
Shape Shoulder
Cast off 10(11:12) sts at beg of next row.
Work 1 row. Cast off rem 10(11:12) sts.

SLEEVES
With 3¼mm (No 10/US 3) needles and M, cast on 49(53:57) sts.
K 5 rows.
Cont in gst and stripes of 2 rows C and 2 rows M **at the same time** inc and work into gst one st at each end of the 3rd and every foll 6th row until there are 69(75:81) sts.
Cont straight until Sleeve measures 16(18:22)cm/6¼(7:8¾)in from cast-on edge, ending with a wrong side row.
Cast off.

TIES (make 2)
With 3¼mm (No 10/US 3) needles cast on 5 sts.
Cont in gst until Tie measures 36(42:48)cm/14(16½:19)in.
Cast off.

TO MAKE UP
Join shoulder seams. Sew on Sleeves. Sew Ties to Fronts level with neck shaping. Join side and Sleeve seams, leaving small opening in left seam level with neck shaping.

Pants
BACK AND FRONT (alike)
With 3¼mm (No 10/US 3) needles and M, cast on 63(69:75)sts.
Cont in gst until work measures 22(27:32)cm/8¾(10½:12½)in from cast-on edge, ending with a wrong side row.
Shape Legs
Next row K28(30:32), k2tog, turn and work on these sts for first leg.
K 3 rows.
Next row K to last 2 sts, k2tog.
Rep the last 4 rows until 27(28:29) sts rem.

Cont straight until work measures 7(9:11)cm/2¾(3½:4¼)in from beg of leg shaping.
Cast off.
With right side facing, join on yarn, cast off 3(5:7) sts, one st on right-hand needle, k1, pass st used to cast off over last st, k to end.
K 3 rows.
Next row Skpo, k to end.
Rep the last 4 rows until 27(28:29) sts rem.
Cont straight until work measures 7(9:11)cm/2¾(3½:4¼)in from beg of leg shaping.
Cast off.

TO MAKE UP
Join side and inner leg seams. Join elastic into a circle, work a herringbone casing over the elastic at waist.

Bootees (make 2)
With 3¼mm (No 10/US 3) needles and M, cast on 36(42:48) sts.
K 1 row.
Cont in gst and stripes of 2 rows C and 2 rows M.
Work 8(12:16) rows.
K 1 row M.
Cont in gst and stripes of 2 rows C and 2 rows M.
Work 12(16:20) rows.
Shape Instep
Next row K24(28:32), turn.
Next row K12(14:16), turn.
Work 26(30:34) rows in gst and stripe patt on centre 12(14:16) sts for instep.
Break off yarn.
Leave sts on a holder.
With right side facing, rejoin yarn at base of instep and with needle holding first sts, pick up and k12(14:16) sts along side of instep, k across centre 12(14:16) sts then pick up and k12(14:16) sts along other side of instep, k rem 12(14:16) sts. 60(70:80) sts.
Cont in gst and stripe patt.
K12(16:20) rows. Break off yarn.
Shape Sole
Next row Slip first 24(28:32) sts onto right-hand needle, rejoin yarn and k12(14:16) sts, turn.
Next row K11(13:15), k2tog, turn.
Rep last row until 12(14:16) sts rem.
Next row [K2tog] to end.
Next row K0(1:0), [k2tog] to end.
Cast off rem 3(4:4) sts.
Join back seam.

Moss Stitch Coathanger

MATERIALS
One 50g ball of Rowan Denim.
Pair of 4mm (No 8/US 6) knitting needles.
6 buttons.
Small amount of wadding to cover coathanger.

MEASUREMENTS
To fit a child's coathanger, 30cm/12in long.

TENSION
20 sts and 30 rows to 10cm/4in over moss st on 4mm (No 8/US 6)
needles before washing.

MAIN PART
With 4mm (No 8/US 6) needles cast on 61 sts.
Moss st row K1, *p1, k1; rep from * to end.
Rep the last row for 12cm/4¾in.
Cast off.

TO MAKE UP
See page 6 for Basic Information on making up Denim yarn.
Cut wadding into 4cm/1½in wide strips, wrap round coathanger to
cover and stitch in place.
With right sides together, fold knitted strip in half lengthways, join
both short ends. Turn to right side. Place over hanger, tack open
edge together 2cm/¾in from cast-on and cast-off edges. Sew on
buttons, evenly spaced through both thicknesses. Remove
tacking.

Moss Stitch Jacket and Bootees

MATERIALS
Jacket: 5(6:7) 50g balls of Rowan Handknit Cotton.
Pair each of 3¾mm (No 9/US 5) and 4mm (No 8/US 6) knitting needles.
6(7:8) buttons.
Bootees: One 50g ball of Rowan Handknit Cotton.
Pair each of 3¾mm (No 9/US 5) and 4mm (No 8/US 6) knitting needles.

MEASUREMENTS
Jacket

To fit ages	3-6	6-12	12-18 months	
Actual measurements				
Chest	59	67	74	cm
	23½	26½	29¼	in
Length to shoulder	26	32	35	cm
	10¼	12½	13¾	in
Sleeve length	14	18	22	cm
	5½	7	8¾	in

Bootees

To fit ages	3 months

TENSION
20 sts and 36 rows to 10cm/4in over moss st on 4mm (No 8/US 6) needles.

Jacket
BACK
With 3¾mm (No 9/US 5) needles cast on 57(65:71) sts.
K 7 rows.
Change to 4mm (No 8/US 6) needles.
Moss st row (right side) K1, *p1, k1; rep from * to end.
Work straight in moss st until Back measures 26(32:35)cm/10¼ (12½:13¾)in from cast-on edge.
Shape Shoulders
Cast off 8(9:10) sts at beg of next 2 rows and 8(10:11) sts at beg of foll 2 rows.
Cast off rem 25(27:29) sts.

POCKET LININGS (make 2)
With 4mm (No 8/US 6) needles cast on 15 sts.
Moss st row (right side) K1, *p1, k1; rep from * to end.
Rep the last row 17 times more.
Leave sts on a holder.

LEFT FRONT
With 3¾mm (No 9/US No 5) needles cast on 33(37:41) sts.

K 7 rows.
Change to 4mm (No 8/US 6) needles and patt.
Next row (right side) P1, *k1, p1; rep from * to last 4 sts, k4.
Next row K4, moss st to end.
Keeping 4 sts at front in gst and remainder in moss st, work a further 16 rows.
Place Pocket
Next row (right side) Moss st 7(9:11) sts, slip next 15 sts onto a holder, patt across 15 sts of Pocket lining, moss st 7(9:11), k4.
Cont in patt until Front measures 22(27:29)cm/8¾(10¾:11½)in from cast-on edge, ending with a wrong side row.
Shape Neck
Next row Patt to last 8(9:10) sts, turn and leave these sts on a holder.
Dec one st at neck edge on every row until 16(19:21) sts rem.

Work straight until Front matches the same as Back to shoulder, ending at side edge.

Shape Shoulder
Cast off 8(9:10) sts at beg of next row.
Work 1 row.
Cast off rem 8(10:11) sts.

RIGHT FRONT
Mark position of buttons, the first one 2cm/¾in from cast-on edge, the 6th(7th:8th) 1cm/½in from neck edge, the remaining 4(5:6) spaced evenly between.
Work to match Left Front, reversing shapings, position of front band and pocket placing, working buttonholes as folls:
Buttonhole row (right side) K1, k2tog, yf, k1, moss st to end.

POCKET TOPS
With 3¾mm (No 9/US 5) needles and right side facing, k across 15 sts of Pocket.
K 3 rows.
Cast off.

SLEEVES
With 3¾mm (No 9/US 5) needles cast on 32(36:42) sts.
K 7 rows.
Change to 4mm (No 8/US 6) needles.
Work in moss st, inc one st at each end of the 7th and every foll 5th(5th:6th) row until there are 46(54:60) sts.
Cont straight until Sleeve measures 14(18:22)cm/5½ (7:8¾)in from cast-on edge, ending with a wrong side row.
Cast off.

COLLAR
Join shoulder seams.
With 3¾mm (No 9/US 5) needles and right side facing, slip 8(9:10) sts from Right Front onto a needle, pick up and k14(16:18) sts up right side of Front neck, 25(27:29) sts across Back neck, 14(16:18) sts down left side of Front neck, k8(9:10) sts from holder. 69(77:85) sts.
Cont in gst. K 1 row.
Cast off 3 sts at beg of next 2 rows. 63(71:79) sts.
Row 1 K48(53:58) sts, turn.
Row 2 K33(35:37) sts, turn.
Row 3 K37(39:41) sts, turn.
Row 4 K41(43:45) sts, turn.
Work 4(4:6) more rows as set, working an extra 4 sts on each row.
Next row K to end.
Next row K2, m1, k to last 2 sts, m1, k2.
K 5 rows.
Rep the last 6 rows twice more. Cast off.

TO MAKE UP
Sew on Sleeves. Join side and Sleeve seams. Sew down Pocket Linings and Pocket Tops. Sew on buttons.

Bootees
With 3¾mm (No 9/US 5) needles cast on 19 sts.
K 1 row.
Next row (right side) K1, m1, k8, m1, k1, m1, k8, m1, k1.
K 1 row.
Next row K1, m1, k10, m1, k1, m1, k10, m1, k1.
K 1 row.
Next row K1, m1, k12, m1, k1, m1, k12, m1, k1.
K 1 row.
Next row K1, m1, k14, m1, k1, m1, k14, m1, k1.
Change to 4mm (No 8/US 6) needles.
Moss st row (wrong side) K1, *p1, k1; rep from * to end.
Rep the last row 7 times more, ending with a right side row.
K 3 rows.
Next row K20, skpo, turn.
Next row Sl 1pwise, [k1, p1] twice, k1, p2tog, turn.
Next row Sl 1pwise, moss st 5, skpo, turn.
Rep these 2 rows 4 times more, then first row again.
Next row Sl 1pwise, moss st 5, k to end. 23 sts.
Work 3 rows moss st, beg each row p1.
Change to 3¾mm (No 9/US 5) needles.
Work 2.5cm/1in single rib, ending with a right side row.
Next row K11, cast off next st, k to end.
K 9 rows on last set of sts.
Cast off.
With right side facing, rejoin yarn to rem sts.
K 9 rows. Cast off.
Join seam, reversing seam for cuff.

Scandinavian Blanket

MATERIALS
Eight 50g balls of Jaeger Matchmaker Merino DK in Main Colour (M). One ball in Contrast Colour (C).
Pair each of 3¼mm (No 10/US 3) and 3¾mm (No 9/US 5) knitting needles.

MEASUREMENTS
Approximately 77cm/30¼in wide by 105cm/41¼in long.

TENSION
24 sts and 32 rows to 10cm/4in over st st on 3¾mm (No 9/US 5) needles.

CHART
When working from chart, odd rows are k rows and read from right to left, even rows are p rows and read from left to right. When working colour motifs, use separate small balls of C for each area of colour and twist yarns on wrong side when changing colour to avoid holes. If desired, the colour motifs can be Swiss darned when knitting is completed (see diagrams on page 7).

Motif A (worked over 23 sts)
Row 1 K to end.
Row 2 P to end.
Rows 3 to 6 Rep rows 1 and 2 twice.
Row 7 K11, p1, k11.
Row 8 P10, k1, p1, k1, p10.
Row 9 K9, p1, [k1, p1] twice, k9.
Row 10 P8, k1, [p1, k1] 3 times, p8.
Row 11 K7, p1, [k1, p1] 4 times, k7.
Row 12 P6, k1, [p1, k1] 5 times, p6.
Row 13 K5, p1, [k1, p1] 6 times, k5.
Row 14 P4, k1, [p1, k1] 7 times, p4.
Rows 15 to 24 Rep rows 13 and 14 five times more.
Row 25 K5, p1, [k1, p1] twice, k3, p1, [k1, p1] twice, k5.
Row 26 P6, k1, p1, k1 p5, k1, p1, k1, p6.
Row 27 K7, p1, k7, p1, k7.
Row 28 P to end.
Rows 29 to 32 Rep rows 1 and 2 twice more.

TO MAKE
With 3¼mm (No 10/US 3) needles and M, cast on 185 sts.
Row 1 P1, *k1, p1; rep from * to end.
Rep this row 3 times more.
Change to 3¾mm (No 9/US 5) needles.
Cont in patt as folls:
Row 1 Moss st 3, patt across row 1 of motif A, moss st 3, patt across row 1 of chart 1, moss st 3, patt across row 1 of motif A, moss st 3, patt across row 1 of chart 2, moss st 3, patt across row 1 of motif A, moss st 3, patt across row 1 of chart 1, moss st

Chart 1 **Chart 2**

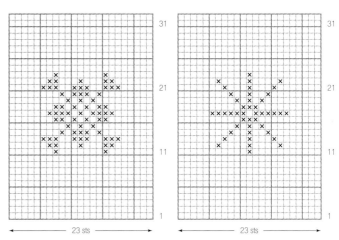

3, patt across row 1 of motif A, moss st 3.
Row 2 Moss st 3, patt across row 2 of motif A, moss st 3, patt across row 2 of chart 1, moss st 3, patt across row 2 of motif A, moss st 3, patt across row 2 of chart 2, moss st 3, patt across row 2 of motif A, moss st 3, patt across row 2 of chart 1, moss st 3, patt across row 2 of motif A, moss st 3.
These 2 rows set the patt.
Rows 3 to 32 Work in patt as set.
Rows 33 to 36 Work 4 rows in moss st.
Row 37 *Moss st 3, k23, moss st 3, patt across row 1 of motif A; rep from * twice more, moss st 3, k23, moss st 3.
Row 38 *Moss st 3, p23, moss st 3, patt across row 2 of motif A; rep from * twice more, moss st 3, p23, moss st 3.
Rows 39 to 68 Work in patt as set.
Rows 69 to 72 Work 4 rows in moss st.
Row 73 Moss st 3, patt across row 1 of motif A, moss st 3, patt across row 1 of chart 2, moss st 3, patt across row 1 of motif A, moss st 3, patt across row 1 of chart 1, moss st 3, patt across row 1 of motif A, moss st 3, patt across row 1 of chart 2, moss st 3, patt across row 1 of motif A, moss st 3.
Row 74 Moss st 3, patt across row 2 of motif A, moss st 3, patt across row 2 of chart 2, moss st 3, patt across row 2 of motif A, moss st 3, patt across row 2 of chart 1, moss st 3, patt across row 2 of motif A, moss st 3, patt across row 2 of chart 2, moss st 3, patt across row 2 of motif A, moss st 3.
Rows 75 to 104 Work in patt as set.
Rows 105 to 108 Work 4 rows in moss st.
Rows 109 to 140 As rows 37 to 68.
Rows 141 to 144 Work 4 rows in moss st.
Rows 145 to 320 Rep rows 1 to 144 once more, then rows 1 to 32 again.
Change to 3¼mm (No 10/US 3) needles.
Work 4 rows in moss st.
Cast off.

TO COMPLETE
With C, make 4 pompons and attach one to each corner.

Scandinavian Jacket

MATERIALS

3(4) 50g balls of Jaeger Matchmaker Merino DK in Cream (M), 1(2) balls in Red and one ball in Black.
Pair each of 3¼mm (No 10/US 3) and 3¾mm (No 9/US 5) knitting needles.
25(30)cm/10(12)in open-ended zip.

MEASUREMENTS

To fit ages	9-12	12-18	months
Actual measurements			
Chest	62	67	cm
	24½	26¼	in
Length to shoulder	30	34	cm
	11¾	3½	in
Sleeve length	18	21	cm
	7	8¼	in

TENSION

24 sts and 32 rows to 10cm/4in over st st on 3¾mm (No 9/US 5) needles.
26 sts and 32 rows to 10cm/4in over patt on 3¾mm (No 9/US 5) needles.

CHARTS

When working from chart, odd rows are k rows and read from right to left, even rows are p rows and read from left to right. When working reindeer motif, use separate small balls of C for each area of colour and twist yarns on wrong side when changing colour to avoid holes.

BACK

With 3¼mm (No 10/US 3) needles and Red, cast on 78(82) sts.
Rib row 1 K2, *p2, k2; rep from * to end.
Rib row 2 P2, *k2, p2; rep from * to end.
Rep the last 2 rows for 4(5)cm/1½(2)in, ending rib row 2 and inc 3(5) sts across last row. 81(87) sts.

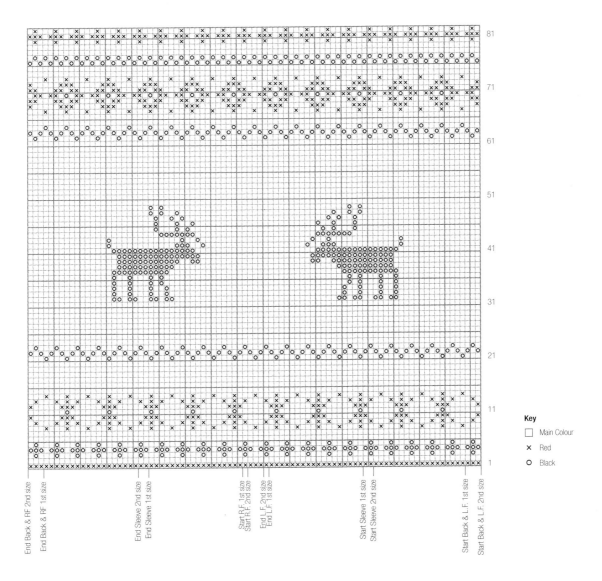

Key

☐ Main Colour
✕ Red
○ Black

Change to 3¾mm (No 9/US 5) needles.
Work in patt from chart to row 61.

2nd size only

With M and beg with a p row, work 4 rows in st st.

Both sizes

Beg at row 62 cont in patt to end of chart.
With M and beg with a k row, work until Back measures
30(34)cm/11¾(13½)in from cast-on edge, ending with a p row.

Shape Shoulders

Cast off 13(14) sts at beg of next 2 rows and 12(13) sts on foll
2 rows.
Leave rem 31(33) sts on a holder.

POCKET LININGS (make 2)

With 3¾mm (No 9/US 5) needles and M, cast on 20 sts.
Beg with a k row, work 15 rows in st st.
Leave sts on a holder.

LEFT FRONT

With 3¼mm (No 10/US 3) needles and Red, cast on 42(46) sts.
Use a small separate ball of Red for 4 sts in gst at centre front.
Rib row 1 K2, *p2, k2; rep from * to last 4 sts, k4.
Rib row 2 K4, p2, *k2, p2; rep from * to end.
Rep the last 2 rows for 4(5)cm/1½(2)in, ending rib row 2.
Change to 3¾mm (No 9/US 5) needles.
Working gst border at front edge in Red, work as folls:
Work in patt from chart to row 16.

Place Pocket

Next row Patt 11(13), then patt next 20 sts and place these sts on
a holder, work to end.
Next row Patt 11(13), patt across Pocket Lining, patt to end.
Cont in patt from chart to row 61.

2nd size only

With M and beg with a p row, work 4 rows in st st.

Both sizes

Beg at row 62 cont in patt until Front measures 26(30)cm/10¼
(12)in from cast-on edge, ending with a wrong side row.

Shape Neck

Next row Patt to last 10(11) sts, leave these sts on a holder.
Working in patt to end of chart, then in st st in M, dec one st at
neck edge on every row until 25(27) sts rem.
Work straight until Front matches Back to shoulder, ending at side
edge.

Shape Shoulder

Cast off 13(14) sts at beg of next row.
Patt 1 row.
Cast off rem 12(13) sts.

RIGHT FRONT

With 3¼mm (No 10/US 3) needles and Red, cast on 42(46) sts.
Use a small separate ball of Red for 4 sts in gst at centre front.
Rib row 1 K6, *p2, k2; rep from * to end.
Rib row 2 P2, *k2, p2; rep from * to last 4 sts, k4.
Rep the last 2 rows for 4(5)cm/1½(2)in, ending rib row 2.
Change to 3¾mm (No 9/US 5) needles.
Working gst border at front edge in Red, work as folls:
Work in patt from chart to row 16.

Place Pocket

Next row Patt 11(13), then patt next 20 sts and place these sts on
a holder, work to end.
Next row Patt 11(13), patt across Pocket Lining, patt to end.
Cont in patt from chart to row 61.

2nd size only

With M and beg with a p row, work 4 rows in st st.

Both sizes

Beg at row 62 cont in patt until Front measures 26(30)cm/10¼
(12)in from cast-on edge, ending with a wrong side row.

Shape Neck

Next row K4 Red, break off all yarns, sl these 4 sts and next 6(7)
sts on a holder, join in yarn, patt to end.
Working in patt to end of chart, then in st st in M, dec one st at
neck edge on every row until 25(27) sts rem.

Work straight until Front matches Back to shoulder, ending at side edge.

Shape Shoulder

Cast off 13(14) sts at beg of next row.

Patt 1 row.

Cast off rem 12(13) sts.

SLEEVES

With 3¼mm (No 10/US 3) needles and Red, cast on 38(42) sts.

Rib row 1 K2, *p2, k2; rep from * to end.

Rib row 2 P2, *k2, p2; rep from * to end.

Rep the last 2 rows for 4(5)cm/1½(2)in, ending rib row 2 and inc 3 sts across last row. 41(45) sts.

Change to 3¾mm (No 9/US 5) needles.

Work rows 1 to 14 from chart, then cont in st st in M only, **at the same time** inc and work into patt one st at each end of 3rd and every foll 4th row until there are 61(65) sts.

Work straight until Sleeve measures 18(21)cm/7(8¼)in from cast-on edge, ending with a wrong side row.

Cast off.

COLLAR

Join shoulder seams.

With 3¼mm (No 10/US 3) needles, right side facing and Red, slip 4 sts from holder onto a needle, k remaining 6(7) sts, pick up and k10(11) sts up Right Front, k 31(33) sts from Back neck holder, pick up and k9(10) sts down left side of Front neck, k10(11) sts from holder. 70(76) sts.

Work in rib with gst border as folls:

Next row K6, *p1, k2; rep from * to last 7 sts, p1, k6.

Row 1 K4, p2, rib 48(52), turn.

Row 2 Rib 37(39) sts, turn.

Row 3 Rib 40(42) sts, turn.

Row 4 Rib 43(45) sts, turn.

Row 5 Rib 46(48) sts, turn.

Row 6 Rib 49(51) sts, turn.

Next row Rib to last 6 sts, p2, k4.

Next row K6, *m1, p1, k2; rep from * to last 7 sts, m1, p1, k6.

Next row K4, *p2, k2; rep from * to last 6 sts, p2, k4.

Next row K6, *p2, k2; rep from * to last 8 sts, p2, k6.

Rep the last 2 rows 6(7) times more.

Cast off in patt.

POCKET TOPS

With 3¼mm (No 10/US 3) needles, right side facing and Red, k across sts on pocket opening.

K 3 rows.

Cast off.

MAKE UP

Join shoulder seams. Sew on Sleeves. Sew down Pocket Linings and row ends of Pocket Tops. Join side and Sleeve seams. Sew in zip.

Bobble Hat

MATERIALS

1(2) 50g balls of Jaeger Matchmaker Merino DK.

Pair each of 3¼mm (No 10/US 3) and 4mm (No 8/US 6) knitting needles.

TENSION

22 sts and 30 rows to 10cm/4in over st st on 4mm (No 8/US 6) needles.

MEASUREMENTS

To fit ages	6-12	18-24	months

TO MAKE

With 4mm (No 8/US 6) needles cast on 98(106) sts.

Rib row 1 K2, *p2, k2; rep from * to end.

Rib row 2 P2, *k2, p2; rep from * to end.

Rep these 2 rows for 4cm/1½in, ending rib row 1.

Change to 3¼mm (No 10/US 3) needles, starting with rib row 1 work in rib for a further 4cm/1½in.

Change to 4mm (No 8/US 6) needles and cont in rib until Hat measures 15(19)cm/6(7½)in from cast-on edge, ending with rib row 2.

Shape Top

Row 1 K2, *p2tog, k2; rep from * to end.

Row 2 P2, *k1, p2; rep from * to end.

Row 3 K2, *p1, k2; rep from * to end.

Row 4 P2, *k1, p2; rep from * to end.

Row 5 K2tog, *p1, k2tog; rep from * to end.

Row 6 P1, *k1, p1; rep from * to end.

Row 7 K1, *p3tog, k1; rep from * to end.

Row 8 P1, *p2tog; rep from * to end.

Break off yarn, thread end through rem sts, pull up and secure.

Join seam reversing seam on last 4cm/1½in.

Make a pompon and sew to top of Hat.

Scottie Dog Cardigan

MATERIALS

6(7) 50g balls of Rowan Cotton Glace in Beige (M). One ball of each in Black, Aqua, White and Dark Red.
Pair each of 2¾mm (No 12/US 2) and 3¼mm (No 10/US 3) knitting needles. One each of 2¾mm (No 12/US 2) and 3¼mm (No 10/US 3) circular knitting needles.
7(8) buttons.

MEASUREMENTS

To fit ages	12-18	24-36	months
Actual measurements			
Chest	66	73	cm
	26	28¾	in
Length to shoulder	30	35	cm
	11¾	13¾	in
Sleeve length	23	26	cm
	9	10¼	in

TENSION

25 sts and 34 rows to 10cm/4in over patt on 3¼mm (No 10/US 3) needles.

CHART

When working from chart, odd rows are k rows and read from right to left, even rows are p rows and read from left to right. When working colour motifs, use separate small balls of each contrast for each area of colour and twist yarns on wrong side when changing colour to avoid holes.

BACK and FRONTS

With 2¾mm (No 12/US 2) circular needle and M, cast on 173(189) sts.
Work backwards and forwards in rows as folls:
Row 1 (right side) K2, *p1, k1; rep from * to last 3 sts, p1, k2.
Row 2 K1, *p1, k1; rep from * to end.
Rep these 2 rows once more.
Buttonhole row Rib 3, yrn, rib 2tog, rib to end.
Cont in rib until work measures 3cm/1¼in, ending rib row 2.
Next row Rib 6, leave these sts on a safety pin, rib to last 6 sts, leave these 6 sts on a safety pin. 161(177) sts.
Change to 3¼mm (No 10/US 3) circular needle and st st.
Work 6(8) rows.
Work 14 rows from chart as folls:
!st size only
Row 1 Working from chart 1 as indicated, k3 sts, work across 28 st patt rep 3 times, then working from chart 2, work across 28 st patt rep twice, then work first 18 sts of this patt rep once more.
2nd size only
Row 1 Working from chart 1 as indicated, k11 sts, work across 28 st patt rep 3 times, then working from chart 2, work across 28 st

patt rep twice, then work first 26 sts of this patt rep once more.
Both sizes
This row sets the position of the patt.
Cont to end of chart.
Cont in st st and M until work measures 16(20)cm/6¼(8)in from cast-on edge, ending with a p row.
Divide for Back and Fronts
Next row K40(44), leave these sts on a holder for Right Front, k until there are 81(89) sts on needle, leave these sts on a holder for Back, k40(44).
Cont on last set of 40(44) sts only for Left Front.
Dec one st at armhole edge on 6(7) foll alt rows. 34(37) sts.
Cont straight until work measures 25(30)cm/9¼(11¾) from cast-on edge, ending at front edge.
Shape Neck
Next row P6(7) sts, place these sts on a holder, p to end.
Dec one st at neck edge on every row until 20(22) sts rem.
Cont straight until work measures 30(35)cm/11¾(13¾)in from cast-on edge, ending at armhole edge.
Shape Shoulder
Cast off 10(11) sts at beg of next row.
P 1 row.
Cast off rem 10(11) sts.
With wrong side facing, work across centre 81(91) sts for Back.
Shape Armholes
Dec one st at armhole edge on next and 5(6) foll alt rows. 69(77) sts.

Cont straight until Back measures same as Front to shoulder shaping, ending with a wrong side row.

Shape Shoulders

Cast off 10(11) sts at beg of next 4 rows.

Leave rem 29(33) sts on a holder.

With wrong side facing, work across last set of 40(44) sts for Right Front.

Complete to match Left Front.

SLEEVES

With 2¾mm (No 12/US 2) needles and M, cast on 46(50) sts.

Row 1 (right side) *K1, p1; rep from * to end.

Rep this row for 4(4.5)cm/1½(1¾)in, ending with a wrong side row. Change to 3¼mm (No 10/US 3) needles.

Work in st st, inc one st at each end of the 3rd and every foll 4th row until there are 72(78) sts.

Cont straight until Sleeve measures 23(26)cm/9(10¼)in from cast-on edge, ending with a wrong side row.

Shape Top

Dec one st at each end of next and 5(6) foll alt rows. 60(64) sts. Cast off.

BUTTON BAND

With 2¾mm (No 12/US 2) needles, right side facing and M, join on yarn to sts on safety pin, cast on one st, rib as set to end. Cont in rib until band fits up Left Front to neck shaping, ending with a

wrong side row. Leave sts on safety pin. Sew band in place. Mark positions for buttons, the first one to match buttonhole already worked, the last to come on 4th row of neckband, and 5(6) more spaced evenly between.

BUTTONHOLE BAND

With 2¾mm (No 12/US 2) needles, wrong side facing and M, join on yarn to sts on safety pin, cast on one st, rib to end. Cont in rib until band fits up Right Front to neck shaping, ending with a wrong side row **at the same time** making buttonholes, as before, to correspond with markers. Sew band in place.

NECKBAND

Join shoulder seams.

With 2¾mm (No 12/US 2) needles, right side facing and M, rib 6 sts from Buttonhole Band, rib next st tog with first st on neck shaping, k rem 5(6) sts, pick up and k14 sts up Right Front to shoulder, k across 29(33) sts of Back neck, pick up and k14 sts down left side of Front neck, k5(6) sts on Front neck shaping, k next st tog with first st of Button Band, rib rem 6 sts. 81(87) sts.

Work 2cm/1in rib as set, working buttonhole on 4th row. Cast off in rib.

TO MAKE UP

Sew in Sleeves. Join side and Sleeve seams. Sew on buttons.

Chart 1

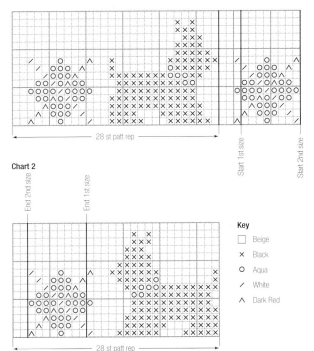

← 28 st patt rep →

Start 1st size

Start 2nd size

Chart 2

End 2nd size

End 1st size

← 28 st patt rep →

Key

☐	Beige
✕	Black
○	Aqua
╱	White
∧	Dark Red

Scottie Dog Cushion

MATERIALS
Two 50g balls of Rowan Cotton Glace in Aqua (M). One ball of each in Black, Dark Red and White.
Pair of 3¼mm (No 10/US 3) knitting needles.
25cm x 25cm/10in x10in cushion pad.

MEASUREMENTS
25cm x 25cm/10in x 10in.

TENSION
25 sts and 34 rows to 10cm/4in over patt on 3¼mm (No 10/US 3) needles.

CHART
When working from chart, odd rows are k rows and read from right to left, even rows are p rows and read from left to right. When working colour motifs, use separate small balls of each contrast for each area of colour and twist yarns on wrong side when changing colour to avoid holes.

BACK
With 3¼mm (No 10/US 3) needles and M, cast on 63 sts.
Row 1 (right side) K1, *p1, k1; rep from * to end.
Rep the last row 3 times more.
Next row [K1, p1] twice, k to last 4 sts, [p1, k1] twice.

Next row K1, p1, k1, p to last 3 sts, k1, p1, k1.
Rep the last 2 rows 37 times more.
Next row K1, *p1, k1; rep from * to end.
Rep the last row 3 times more.
Cast off.

FRONT
With 3¼mm (No 10/US 3) needles and M, cast on 63 sts.
Row 1 (right side) K1, *p1, k1; rep from * to end.
Rep the last row 3 times more.
Next row [K1, p1] twice, k to last 4 sts, [p1, k1] twice.
Next row K1, p1, k1, p to last 3 sts, k1, p1, k1.
Rep the last 2 rows twice more.
Next row With M, [k1, p1] twice, work in patt from chart to last 4 sts, with M, [p1, k1] twice.
Cont to end of chart.
Next row [K1, p1] twice, k to last 4 sts, [p1, k1] twice.
Next row K1, p1, k1, p to last 3 sts, k1, p1, k1.
Rep the last 2 rows twice more.
Next row K1, *p1, k1; rep from * to end.
Rep the last row 3 times more.
Cast off.

TO MAKE UP
With right sides together, join 3 seams. Turn to right side, insert cushion, join remaining seam.

The pattern for the Scottie dog toy included in the photograph opposite is given in *Toy Knits*, also by Debbie Bliss.

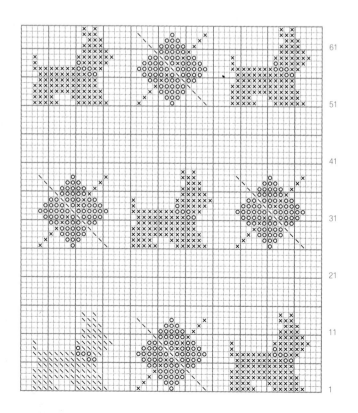

Key

☐ Aqua

✕ Black

○ Dark Red

╲ White

Shawl-collared Tunic with Hat and Shoes

MATERIALS
Tunic: 3(4:5) 50g balls of Rowan Felted Tweed DK. Small amount of Rowan True 4 ply Botany for embroidery.
Pair each of 3¼mm (No 10/US 3) and 4mm (No 8/US 6) knitting needles.
Hat: One 50g ball of Rowan Felted Tweed DK. Small amount of Rowan True 4 ply Botany for embroidery.
Pair each of 2¾mm (No 12/US 2) and 4mm (No 8/US 6) knitting needles.
Shoes: One 50g ball of Rowan Felted Tweed DK. Small amount of Rowan True 4 ply Botany for embroidery.
Pair of 3¼mm (No 10/US 3) knitting needles.

MEASUREMENTS

Tunic

To fit ages	9-12	12-24	24-36	months
Actual measurements				
Chest	64	70	81	cm
	25¼	27½	31¾	in
Length	33	38	45	cm
	13	15	17¾	in
Sleeve length				
with cuff turned back	20	23	28	cm
	8	9	11	in

Hat

To fit ages	9-12	12-24	months

Shoes

To fit	6-12	months

TENSION
21 sts and 36 rows to 10cm/4in over moss st on 4mm (No 8/US 6) needles.

Tunic
BACK
With 4mm (No 8/US 6) needles cast on 67(73:85) sts.
Moss st row K1, *p1, k1; rep from * to end.
Rep the last row until Back measures 33(38:45)cm/13(15:17¾)in from cast-on edge.
Shape Shoulders
Cast off 10(11:14) sts at beg of next 4 rows. 27(29:29) sts.
Shape Collar
Change to 3¼mm (No 10/US 3) needles.
Row 1 Cast on 4 sts, [k1, p1] twice across these 4 sts, moss st to end.

Rows 2 to 16 As row 1. 91(93:93) sts.
Change to 4mm (No 8/US 6) needles.
Row 17 Moss st to end.
Rows 18 and 19 Moss st to last 4 sts, turn.
Rows 20 and 21 Moss st to last 8 sts, turn.
Rows 22 and 23 Moss st to last 12 sts, turn.
Rows 24 and 25 Moss st to last 16 sts, turn.
Rows 26 and 27 Moss st to last 20 sts, turn.
Rows 28 and 29 Moss st to last 24 sts, turn.
Rows 30 and 31 Moss st to last 28 sts, turn.
Rows 32 and 33 Moss st to last 32 sts, turn.
Moss st to end of row.
Cast off in moss st.

FRONT
Work as given for Back until Front measures 26(31:38)cm/10¼ (12¼:15)in from cast-on edge.
Neck Shaping
Next row Patt 29(32:37), turn and work on these sts for first side of neck shaping.
**Dec one st at neck edge on every foll alt row until 20(22:28) sts rem.
Cont straight until Front measures the same as Back to shoulder shaping, ending at side edge.
Shape Shoulder
Cast off 10(11:14) sts at beg of next row.
Work 1 row. Cast off rem 10(11:14) sts.
Join yarn to inside edge of rem sts, cast off 9(9:11) sts, patt to end.
Complete to match first side from ** to end.

SLEEVES
With 4mm (No 8/US 6) needles cast on 33(35:39) sts.
Work 3(3:4)cm/1¼(1¼:1½)in moss st as given for Back.
Change to 3¼mm (No 10/US 3) needles.
Work a further 3(3:4)cm/1¼(1¼:1½)in moss st
Change to 4mm (No 8/US 6) needles.
Cont in moss st **at the same time** inc and work into patt one st at each end of the next and every foll 4th row until there are 55(63:71) sts.
Cont straight until Sleeve measures 23(26:32)cm/9(10¼:12½)in from cast-on edge, ending with a wrong side row.
Cast off.

TO MAKE UP
Join shoulder seams. Sew on Sleeves. Join side and Sleeve seams, reversing seam on top 3(3:4)cm/1¼(1¼:1½)in for cuff. With double length of 4 ply yarn, work in blanket st round lower edge and lower Sleeve edge. Lap right Collar over left and sew edges to neck edge.

Hat

EAR FLAPS (make 2)

With 4mm (No 8/US 6) needles cast on 9 sts.

Moss st row K1, *p1, k1; rep from * to end.

This row forms the moss st patt.

Cont in moss, inc one st at each end of the next and 3(4) foll alt rows. 17(19) sts.

Work 6(10) rows straight.

Dec one st at each end of next row and foll alt row.

Inc one st at each end of 2nd and 2 foll rows. 19(21) sts.

Work 1 row. Leave these sts on a holder.

Main Part

Cast on 11(13) sts, moss st across first flap, cast on 33(35) sts, moss st across second flap, cast on 12(14) sts. 94(106) sts.

Work 35(45) rows moss st.

Shape Top

1st row *Moss st 15(17), work 3tog; rep from * to last 4 sts, moss st 4. 84(94) sts.

Moss st 3 rows.

5th row *Moss st 13(15), work 3tog; rep from * to last 4 sts, moss st 4. 74(84) sts.

Moss st 3 rows.

9th row *Moss st 11(13), work 3tog; rep from * to last 4 sts, moss st 4. 64(74) sts.

Moss st 3 rows.

Cont in this way dec 10 sts on the next and every foll 4th row until 34 sts rem for both sizes.

Next and every foll alt row Moss st to end.

Next row [Moss st 7, work 3tog, moss st 7] twice.

Next row [Moss st 6, work 3tog, moss st 6] twice.

Next row [Moss st 5, work 3tog, moss st 5] twice.

Next row [Moss st 4, work 3tog, moss st 4] twice.

Next row [Moss st 3, work 3tog, moss st 3] twice.

Change to 2¾mm (No 12/US 2) needles.

Cont in moss st on these 14 sts for 3cm/1¼in.

Break off yarn thread through rem sts, pull up and secure, then join back seam.

With double length of 4ply yarn, work in blanket st round edge.

Shoes (make 2)

With 3¼mm (No 10/US 3) needles cast on 36 sts.

Moss st row 1 *P1, k1; rep from * to end.

Moss st row 2 *K1, p1; rep from * to end.

Rep the last 2 rows for 8cm/3in from cast-on edge, ending row 2.

Shape Instep

Next row K12, moss st 12, turn.

Next row Moss st 12, turn.

Work 24 rows in moss st on centre 12 sts for instep.

Break off yarn.

With right side facing, rejoin yarn at base of instep and pick up and k12 sts along side of instep, k across centre 12 sts then pick up and k12 sts along other side of instep, k rem 12 sts. 60 sts.

K 6 rows.

Next row (wrong side) [Pick up st 5 rows below corresponding with next st on left-hand needle and k them tog] to end.

Work 12 rows in moss st. Break off yarn.

Shape Sole

Next row Slip first 24 sts onto right-hand needle, rejoin yarn and k12 sts, turn.

Next row K11, k2tog, turn.

Rep last row until 12 sts rem.

Next row [K2tog] to end.

Cast off rem 6 sts.

Join back seam, reversing seam on top 3cm/1¼in for cuff. Turn back cuff.

With double length of 4 ply yarn, work in blanket st round cuff edge.

Patchwork Blanket

MATERIALS

Two 50g balls of Rowan Wool Cotton in each of Lilac (L), Red (R), Blue (B), Maroon (M), Green (G), Yellow (Y), Navy (N) and Cream (C).
Pair of 3¾mm (No 9/US 5) knitting needles.
Medium size crochet hook.

MEASUREMENTS

Approximately 72cm/28¼in wide by 92cm/36¼in long.

TENSION

23 sts and 41 rows to 10cm/4in over gst on 3¾mm (No 9/US 5) needles.

BLANKET
ONE SQUARE

With 3¾mm (No 9/US 5) needles and L, cast on 23 sts.
K 41 rows.
Cast off.

L = Lilac	G = Green
R = Red	Y = Yellow
B = Blue	N = Navy
M = Maroon	C = Cream

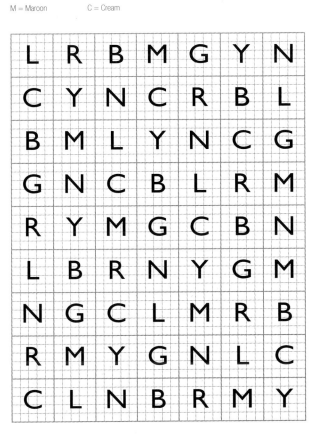

Make 7 more squares in L, 8 in R, 8 in B, 8 in M, 7 in G, 7 in Y, 9 in N, 8 in C.

TO MAKE UP

Using plan, join squares together to form blanket.

Crochet Edging: With crochet hook and right side facing, join L to centre of side edge.

Round 1 1 chain, [work in double crochet to corner, 3 double crochet in corner] 4 times, work in double crochet to first double crochet, slip stitch in first double crochet. Fasten off.

Round 2 Attach R to next double crochet, 1 chain, [work in double crochet to corner, 3 double crochet in corner] 4 times, work in double crochet to first double crochet, slip stich in first double crochet. Fasten off.

Rounds 3 to 5 Working one round each of B, C and M, work as round 2.

Nellie the Sheep

MATERIALS
Two 50g balls of Rowan Wool Cotton in Cream (C), One ball in Black (B).
Pair of 3mm (No 11/US 2) knitting needles.
Stuffing.

TENSION
28 sts and 46 rows to 10cm/4in over moss st on 3mm (No 11/US 2) needles.

UPPER BODY
Right Back Leg
With 3mm (No 11/US 2) needles and C, cast on 18 sts.
Place a marker between 12th and 13th sts.
Row 1 (right side) *K1, p1; rep from * to end.
Row 2 *P1, k1; rep from * to end.
These 2 rows set the moss st patt.
Cast on 8 sts at beg of next row.
Inc one st at beg of next row and at same edge on 3 foll 3rd rows. 30 sts.
Moss st 2 rows.
Leave these sts on a holder.

Left Back Leg
With C, cast on 18 sts.
Place a marker between 6th and 7th sts.
Row 1(wrong side) *K1, p1; rep from * to end.
Row 2 *P1, k1; rep from * to end.
These 2 rows set the moss st patt.
Next row Cast on 8 sts moss st to last st, work twice in last st.
Work 2 rows.
Inc one st at beg of next row and at same edge on 2 foll 3rd rows. 30 sts.
Moss st 2 rows.
Next row Moss st to last st, work twice in last st, then moss st across sts on holder.
61 sts.
Work 10 rows straight.
Cast off 8 sts at beg of next 2 rows. 45 sts.
Work 14 rows straight.
Front Legs
Cast on 8 sts at beg of next 2 rows. 61 sts.
Work 9 rows straight.
Shape Back Head
Next row Patt 31, turn, leave rem 30 sts on a holder.
Inc one st at end of 4 foll alt rows, then at same edge on 5 foll rows. 40 sts.
Cast off 8 sts at beg of next row. 32 sts.
Work 1 row.
Inc one st at end of next row.
Work 2 rows straight.

Dec one st at end of next row and at same edge on 3 foll rows. 29 sts.
Work 1 row.
Cast off 5 sts at beg of next row and foll alt row.
Mark outside edge of rem 19 sts.
Cast off.
With wrong side facing, rejoin yarn to sts on holder, work twice in first st, patt to end.
Inc one st at beg of 4 foll alt rows, then at same edge on 4 foll rows. 39 sts.
Next row Cast off 8 sts, patt to last st, work twice in last st. 32 sts.
Work 2 rows.
Inc one st at beg of next row.
Work 2 rows straight.
Dec one st at beg of next row and at same edge on 3 foll rows. 29 sts.

Cast off 5 sts at beg of next row and foll alt row. 19 sts.

Work 1 row.

Mark end of last row.

Cast off.

UNDERSIDE

Back Gusset

With 3mm (No 11/US 2) needles and C, cast on 3 sts.

Row 1 P1, *k1, p1; rep from * to end.

This row sets the moss st.

Inc one st at each end of the 2nd and 4 foll 4th rows. 13 sts.

Patt 1 row.

Shape Back Legs

**Cast on 8 sts at beg of next 2 rows. 29 sts.

Next row Patt 8, k3tog tbl, patt 7, k3tog, patt 8.

Work 3 rows.

Next row Patt 8, k3tog tbl, patt 3, k3tog, patt 8.

Work 3 rows.

Next row Patt 9, p3tog, patt 9.

Work 3 rows.

Next row Patt 9, p into front, k into back, p into front of next st, patt 9.

Work 3 rows.

Next row Patt 8, *k into front, p into back, k into front of next st *, patt 3; rep from * to *, patt 8.

Work 3 rows.

Next row Patt 8, *k into front, p into back, k into front of next st *, patt 7, rep from * to *, patt 8.

Work 1 row.

Cast off 8 sts at beg of next 2 rows. 13 sts.**

Work 14 rows straight.

Shape Front Legs

Work as given for Back Legs from ** to **.

Dec one st at each end of 5th row and 3 foll 6th rows.

Work 3 rows.

Cast off.

HEAD

With 3mm (No 11/US 2) needles and B, cast on 15 sts.

Beg with a k row, work in st st for 2 rows.

Cont in st st, inc one st at each end of the next row and 3 foll alt rows. 23 sts.

Work 1 row.

Next row Inc in first st, k3, m1, k1, m1, k13, m1, k1, m1, k3, inc in last st.

Work 1 row.

Inc one st at each end of next row.

Work 1 row.

Next row Cast on 2 sts, k these 2 sts, then k7, m1, k1, m1, k15, m1, k1, m1, k7.

Cast on 2 sts at beg of next row. 39 sts.

Mark each end of last row.

Work 2 rows.

Next row K8, k2tog, k1, skpo, k13, k2tog, k1, skpo, k8.

Work 1 row.

Next row K7, k2tog, k1, skpo, k11, k2tog, k1, skpo, k7.

Work 1 row.

Next row K6, k2tog, k1, skpo, k9, k2tog, k1, skpo, k6.

Next row P5, p2tog, p1, p2tog, p7, p2tog, p1, p2tog, p5.

Next row K4, k2tog, k1, skpo, k5, k2tog, k1, skpo, k4.

Cast off.

FEET (make 4)

With 3mm (No 11/US 2) needles and B, cast on 17 sts.

Beg with a k row, work 10 rows in st st.

Inc one st at each end of the next 3 rows. 23 sts.

Work 2 rows.

Next row P1, *p2tog; rep from * to end.

Next row *K2tog; rep from * to end. 6 sts.

Break off yarn, thread through rem sts, pull up and secure.

EARS (make 4)

With 3mm (No 11/US 2) needles and B, cast on 6 sts.

Beg with a k row, work 2 rows in st st.

Next row K3, m1, k3.

Work 3 rows.

Next row K3, m1, k1, m1, k3.

Work 1 row.

Next row K4, m1, k1, m1, k4. 11 sts.

Work 1 row.

Next row K1, skpo, k5, k2tog, k1.

Work 1 row.

Next row K1, skpo, k3, k2tog, k1.

Work 1 row.

Next row K1, skpo, k1, k2tog, k1.

Work 1 row.

Next row K1, s1 1, k2tog, psso, k1.

Cast off rem 3 sts.

TAIL

With 3mm (No 11/US 2) needles and C, cast on 20 sts.

Beg with a k row, work 4 rows in st st.

Cast off.

TO MAKE UP

Join feet back seams and stuff. Placing cast-on edge of underside in line with markers at back of body and cast-off edge in line with markers at front and matching legs, sew underside to body. Join remaining back and top seam at back of body. Gather row end edge of each leg and pull up slightly to fit top of foot. Sew in feet. Join back head seam. Stuff body. Join underchin seam of head from marker to cast-off edge, then with seam at centre, join cast-off edge. Stuff head. Sew head in place, stuffing as necessary. Join paired ear pieces together and sew them in position. Sew together cast-on and cast-off edges of tail. Make a small tassel at one end, sew other end in place. With C, embroider face features.

Throw with Pockets

MATERIALS
Seventeen 50g balls of Rowan Denim.
Pair of 4mm (No 8/US 6) knitting needles.
3 buttons.

MEASUREMENTS
76cm x 86cm/30in x 34in after washing.

TENSION
20 sts and 30 rows to 10cm/4in over moss st on 4mm (No 8/US 6) needles before washing.

MAIN PART
With 4mm (No 8/US 6) needles cast on 141 sts.
K 9 rows.
Inc row K7, [k twice in next st, k13] 9 times, k twice in next st, k7. 151 sts.
Next row K6, p1, *k1, p1; rep from * to last 6 sts, k6.
Rep the last row until work measures 105cm/41½in from cast-on edge.
Dec row K7, [k2tog, k13] 9 times, k2tog, k7. 141 sts.

K 9 rows.
Cast off.

POCKET
With 4mm (No 8/US 6) needles cast on 80 sts.
Work in gst (every row k) until Pocket measures 35cm/13¾in from cast-on edge.
Buttonhole row K13, [cast off 2, k until there are 24 sts on needle] twice, cast off 2, k to end.
Next row K to end, casting on 2 sts over those cast off in previous row.
K 7 rows.
Cast off, placing marker between 52nd and 53rd sts.

TO MAKE UP
See page 6 for Basic Instructions on making up Denim yarn.
Place cast-on edge of Pocket just above garter st edging of main part centrally and sew in position. Beginning at marker and stitching through both thicknesses, divide Pocket into two parts.
Sew on buttons.

Sheep Jacket

MATERIALS
4(5:6) 50g balls of Rowan Wool Cotton in Grey (M), Two balls in Cream (C). One ball each in Blue and Black.
Pair each of 3¾mm (No 9/US 5) and 4mm (No 8/US 6) knitting needles. 25(30:30)cm/10(10:12)in open-ended zip.

MEASUREMENTS

To fit ages	12	24	36	months
Actual measurements				
Chest	72	76	80	cm
	28¼	30	31½	in
Length to shoulder	33	36	40	cm
	13	14¼	15½	in
Sleeve length	21	23	25	cm
	8¼	9	10	in

TENSION
22 sts and 30 rows to 10cm/4in over st st on 4mm (No 8/US 6) needles.

CHARTS
When working from chart, odd rows are k rows and read from right to left, even rows are p rows and read from left to right. When working sheep motifs, use separate small balls of C for each area of colour and twist yarns on wrong side when changing colour to avoid holes.

BACK
With 3¾mm (No 9/US 5) needles and M, cast on 82(86:90) sts.
Rib row 1 K2, *p2, k2; rep from * to end.
Rib row 2 P2, *k2, p2; rep from * to end.
Rep the last 2 rows once more, work 2 rows Black and 4 rows M.
Change to 4mm (No 8/US 6) needles and patt.
With M and beg with a k row, work 2(4:6) rows in st st.
Work 12 rows in patt from chart 1.
With M and beg with a k row, work 8(10:12) rows in st st.
Work 7 rows in patt from chart 2.
With M and beg with a p row, work 5(7:9) rows in st st.
Next row K14(16:17)M, work across row 1 of chart 3, k14(14:16)M, work across row 1 of chart 4, k14(16:17)M.
Next row P14(16:17)M, work across row 2 of chart 4, p14(14:16)M, work across row 2 of chart 3, p14(16:17)M.
Cont as set to end of charts 3 and 4.
With M and beg with a k row, work 8(10:12) rows in st st.
Work 7 rows in patt from chart 2.
With M and beg with a p row, work 9(11:13) rows in st st.
Work 8 rows in patt from chart 5.
With M and beg with a k row, work 4 rows in st st.
Shape Shoulders
Cast off 13(13:14) sts at beg of next 2 rows and 12(13:13) sts on

foll 2 rows.
Cast off rem 32(34:36) sts.

POCKET LININGS (make 2)
With 4mm (No 8/US 6) needles and M, cast on 20 sts.
Beg with a k row, work 15(17:19) rows in st st.
Leave sts on a holder.

LEFT FRONT
With 3¾mm (No 9/US 5) needles and M, cast on 42(42:46) sts.
Use a small separate ball of M for 4 sts in gst at centre front.
Rib row 1 K2, *p2, k2; rep from * to last 4 sts, k4.
Rib row 2 K4, p2, *k2, p2; rep from * to end.
Rep the last 2 rows once more, work 2 rows Black and 4 rows M, inc 2 sts evenly across last row *on 2nd size only*. 42(44:46) sts.
Change to 4mm (No 8/US 6) needles and patt.
Working gst border at front edge in M, work as folls:
With M and beg with a k row, work 2(4:6) rows in st st.
Work 12 rows in patt from chart 1.
With M and beg with a k row, work 2(2:4) rows in st st.
Place Pocket
Next row K13(14:15), then k next 20 sts and place these sts on a holder, k to end.
Next row K4, p5(6:7), p across Pocket Lining, p to end.
With M and beg with a k row, work 4(6:6) rows in st st.
Work 7 rows in patt from chart 2.
With M and beg with a p row, work 5(7:9) rows in st st.
Next row K14(16:17)M, work across row 1 of chart 3, k8(8:9)M.
Next row K4M, p4(4:5)M, work across row 2 of chart 3, p14(16:17)M.
Cont as set to end of chart 3.
With M and beg with a k row, work 8(10:12) rows in st st.
Work 7 rows in patt from chart 2.
Shape Neck
Working in patt to match Back, shape neck as folls:
Next row Patt to last 4 sts, turn, leaving these sts on a safety pin
Dec one st at neck edge on every row until 25(26:27) sts rem.
Cont without further shaping until Front measures same as Back to shoulder, ending at side edge.
Shape Shoulder
Cast off 13(13:14) sts at beg of next row.
Patt 1 row.
Cast off rem 12(13:13) sts.

RIGHT FRONT
With 3¾mm (No 9/US 5) needles and M, cast on 42(42:46) sts.
Use a small separate ball of M for 4 sts in gst at centre front.
Rib row 1 K6, *p2, k2; rep from * to end.
Rib row 2 P2, *k2, p2; rep from * to last 4 sts, k4.
Rep the last 2 rows once more, work 2 rows Black and 4 rows M, inc 2 sts evenly across last row *on 2nd size only*. 42(44:46) sts.
Change to 4mm (No 8/US 6) needles and patt.
Working gst border at front edge in M, work as folls:

Chart 1

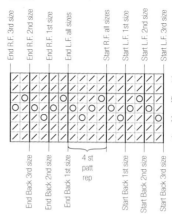

**Key for Charts
1,2 & 5**

☐ M

✕ Blue

○ Black

╱ Cream

Chart 2

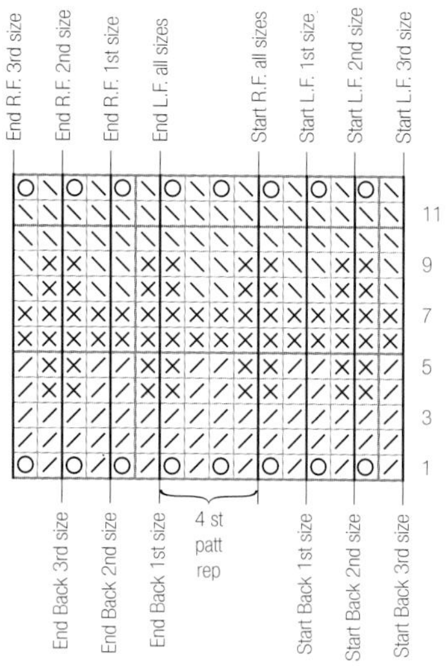

Chart 3

**Key for Charts
3 & 4**

⋀ With C
P on right side
K on wrong side

● With C
P on wrong side
K on right side

○ Black

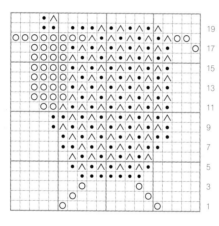

Chart 4

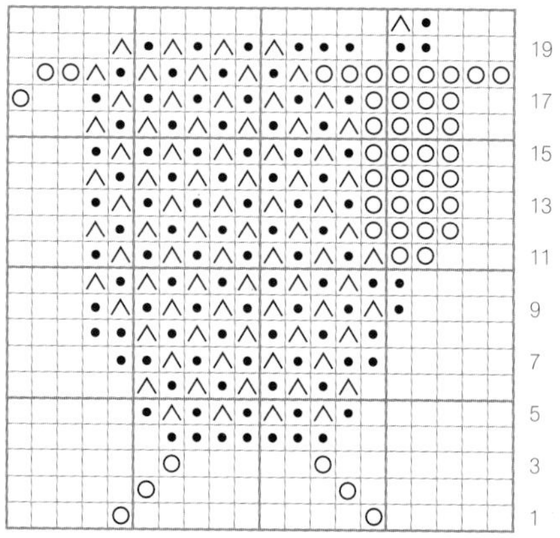

Chart 5

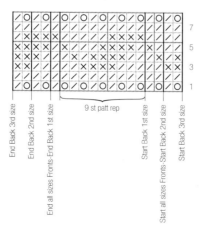

With M and beg with a k row, work 2(4:6) rows in st st.

Work 12 rows in patt from chart 1.

With M and beg with a k row, work 2(2:4) rows in st st.

Place Pocket

Next row K9(10:11), then k next 20 sts and place these sts on a holder, k to end.

Next row P13(14:15), p across Pocket Lining, p to last 4 sts, k4.

Work 7 rows in patt from chart 2.

With M and beg with a k row, work 4(6:6) rows in st st.

With M and beg with a p row, work 5(7:9) rows in st st.

Next row K8(8:9)M, work across row 1 of chart 4, k14(16:17)M.

Next row P14(16:17)M, work across row 2 of chart 4, p4(4:5)M, k4M.

Cont as set to end of chart 4.

With M and beg with a k row, work 8(10:12) rows in st st.

Work 7 rows in patt from chart 2.

Complete to match Left Front.

LEFT SLEEVE

With 3¾mm (No 9/US 5) needles and M, cast on 38(42:46) sts.

Rib row 1 K2, *p2, k2; rep from * to end.

Rib row 2 P2, *k2, p2; rep from * to end.

Rep the last 2 rows once more.

Work 2 rows Black and 4 rows M.

Change to 4mm (No 8/US 6) needles.

Work in patt inc one st at each end every foll 4th row until there are 60(66:72) sts *at the same time* work in patt as folls:

With M and beg with a k row, work 2 rows in st st.

Work 7 rows in patt from chart 2, placing patt as given for Back.

With M and beg with a p row, work 5(7:9) rows in st st. 44(50:54) sts.

Next row K12(15:17)M, work across row 1 of chart 3, k12(15:17)M.

This row sets position of chart.

Cont inc as set to end of chart 3.

With M and beg with a k row, work 8(10:12) rows in st st.

Work 7 rows in patt from chart 2.

With M and beg with a p row, work 3(5:7) rows in st st.

Cast off.

RIGHT SLEEVE

Work as given for Left Sleeve, working from chart 4 instead of chart 3.

LEFT COLLAR

With 3¾mm (No 9/US 5) needles, right side facing and M, k across 4 sts on Left Front band.

K 1 row.

Cont in gst *at the same time* inc one st at each end of the next and 2 foll 4th rows.

K 2 rows.

Working 6 rows Black, 6 rows M and 6 rows Black, then cont in M inc as set until there are 26 sts, ending right side of jacket and wrong side of Collar facing.

Shape Collar

** **Next 2 rows** K14, sl 1, turn k to end.

K 4 rows **.

Rep from ** to ** 7 times. Cast off.

RIGHT COLLAR

With 3¾mm (No 9/US 5) needles and wrong side facing, rejoin M to inner edge, k across 4 sts on Right Front band.

Cont in gst *at the same time* inc one st at each end of the next and 2 foll 4th rows.

K 2 rows.

Working 6 rows Black, 6 rows M and 6 rows Black, then cont in M inc as set until there are 26 sts.

K 1 row, ending right side of jacket and wrong side of Collar facing.

Shape Collar

Next 2 rows K14, sl 1, turn k to end.

K 4 rows **.

Rep from ** to ** 7 times. Cast off.

POCKET TOPS

With 3¾mm (No 9/US 5) needles, right side facing and M, k across sts on pocket opening.

K 3 rows.

Cast off.

TO MAKE UP

Join shoulder seams. Join back seam of Collar, then sew to neck edge. Sew on Sleeves. Sew down Pocket Linings and row ends of Pocket Tops. Join side and Sleeve seams. Sew in zip.

Stocking Stitch Sweater

MATERIALS
6(6:7) 50g balls of Rowan all seasons cotton.
Pair of 4½mm (No 7/US 7) knitting needles.

MEASUREMENTS

To fit ages	1	2	3	years
Actual measurements				
Chest	62	70	78	cm
	24½	27½	30¾	in
Length	30	35	40	cm
	11¾	13¾	15¾	in
Sleeve length	19	22	25	cm
	7½	8¾	10	in

TENSION
18 sts and 25 rows to 10cm/4in over st st on 4½mm (No 7/US 7) needles.

BACK and FRONT (both alike)
With 4½mm (No 7/US 7) needles cast on 56(63:70) sts.
Beg with a k row, work in st st until work measures 17(20:23)cm/6¾(7¾:9)in from cast-on edge, ending with a p row.
Shape Raglan Armholes
Row 1 K3, skpo, k to last 5 sts, k2tog, k3.
Row 2 P to end.
Rep the last 2 rows until 22(25:28) sts rem, ending with a p row.
Beg with a k row, work 12 rows st st.
Cast off.

SLEEVES
With 4½ mm (No 7/US 7) needles cast on 34(37:40) sts.
Work in st st, inc one st at each end of the 3rd and every foll 6th row until there are 46(51:56) sts.
Cont straight until sleeve measures 19(22:25)cm/7½(8¾:10)in from cast-on edge, ending with a wrong side row.
Shape Raglan Top
Row 1 K3, skpo, k to last 5 sts, k2tog, k3.
Row 2 P to end.
Rep the last 2 rows until 12(13:14) sts rem, ending with a p row.
Beg with a k row, work 12 rows st st.
Cast off.

TO MAKE UP
Join raglan seams. Join side and Sleeve seams.

Striped Jacket

MATERIALS

One 50g ball each of Rowan Cotton 4 ply in Pink (A), Rust (B), White (C), Green (D), Light Blue (E), Blue (F), Navy (G) and Beige (H).
Pair each of 2¼mm (No 13/US 1) and 2¾mm (No 12/US 2) knitting needles.
6(6:7) buttons.

MEASUREMENTS

To fit ages	6	9	12	months
Actual measurements				
Chest	56	62	70	cm
	22	24½	27½	in
Length to shoulder	26	30	33	cm
	10¼	12	13	in
Sleeve length				
(with cuff turned back)	16	18	20	cm
	6¼	7	8	in

TENSION

25 sts and 50 rows to 10cm/4in over gst on 2¾mm (No 12/US 2) needles.

BACK AND FRONTS

With 2¼mm (No 13/US 1) needles and A, cast on 140(156:176) sts.
K 3 rows.
Change to 2¾mm (No 12/US 2) needles and stripe patt.
K 2 rows B, 2 rows C, 4 rows D, 6 rows E, 4 rows F, 2 rows G, 4 rows H and 4 rows A.
Cont straight in gst until work measures 15(17:19)cm/6(6¾:7½)in from cast-on edge, ending with a wrong side row.

Divide for Back and Fronts

Next row K35(39:44), leave these sts on a holder for Right Front, k next 70(78:88), leave these sts on a holder for Back, k to end.

Left Front

Work straight on last set of 35(39:44) sts until Front measures 22(25:27)cm/8¾(9¾:10½)in from cast-on edge, ending at neck edge.

Shape Neck

Next row K8(9:10) sts, leave these sts on a safety pin, k to end.
Dec one st at neck edge on every row until 18(20:22) sts rem.
Work straight until Front measures 26(30:33)cm/10¼(12:13)in from cast-on edge, ending at armhole edge.

Shape Shoulder

Cast off 9(10:11) sts at beg of next row.
Work 1 row.
Cast off rem 9(10:11) sts.

BACK

With wrong side facing, rejoin yarn to next st.
Work straight until work measures same as Left Front to shoulder, ending with a wrong side row.

Shape Shoulders

Cast off 9(10:11) sts at beg of next 4 rows.
Leave rem 34(38:44) sts on a spare needle.

Right Front

With wrong side facing, rejoin yarn to next st, work to match Left Front, reversing all shapings.

SLEEVES

With 2¾mm (No 12/US 2) needles and F, cast on 40(43:46) sts.
K 3 rows F, 6 rows E, 4 rows D, 2 rows C.
K 3 rows B to reverse stripe patt.
Cont in stripes of 2 rows C, 4 rows D, 6 rows E, 4 rows F, 2 rows G, 4 rows H, 4 rows A, 2 rows B, **at the same time** inc and work into patt one st at each end of the next and every foll 6th row until there are 56(65:72) sts.
Cont straight until Sleeve measures 20(22:24)cm/8(8¼:9½) from cast-on edge, ending with a wrong side row.
Cast off.

NECKBAND

Join shoulder seams.
With 2¾mm (No 12/US 2) needles and right side facing, sl 8(9:10) sts from safety pin, join in A, pick up and k13(16:19) sts up Right Front neck edge, k across 34(38:44) sts on Back neck, pick up

and k13(16:19) sts down left side of Front neck, k8(9:10) sts from safety pin. 76(88:102) sts.

K 3 rows.

Cast off.

BUTTON BAND

With 2¾mm (No 12/US 2) needles, right side facing and A, pick up and k57(65:70) sts along Left Front edge.

K 3 rows.

Cast off.

BUTTONHOLE BAND

With 2¾mm (No 12/US 2) needles, right side facing and A, pick up and k57(65:70) sts along Right Front edge.

K 1 row.

Buttonhole row K3(4:4) sts, [k2tog, yf, k8(9:8) sts] 5(5:6) times, k2tog, yf, k2(4:4).

K 1 row.

Cast off.

TO MAKE UP

Join Sleeve seams, reversing seam on cuff for 4cm/1¾in. Sew in Sleeves. Sew on buttons.

Striped Cushion

MATERIALS
One 50g ball each of Rowan Handknit Cotton in Mid Green (A), Grey (B), Gold (C), Purple (D), Wine (E) and Light Green (F). Small amount in Black (G), Cream (H) and Stone (I).
Pair of 4mm (No 8/US 6) knitting needles.
25cm x 25 cm/10in x10in cushion pad.

MEASUREMENTS
23cm x 23cm/9in x 9in.

TENSION
20 sts and 40 rows to 10cm/4in over gst on 4mm (No 8/US 6) needles.

TO MAKE
With 4mm (No 8/US 6) needles and A, cast on 46 sts.
K 3 rows.
**K 6 rows B, 4 rows C, 2 rows H, 2 rows G, 6 rows D, 2 rows E, 2 rows I, 4 rows F, 4 rows A.
Rep from ** 4 times more.
K 6 rows B, 4 rows C, 2 rows H, 2 rows G, 6 rows D, 17 rows E.
Cast off.

TO MAKE UP
Leaving last 17 rows free, with right sides together, join side seams. Turn to right side, fold last 17 rows to inside.

Striped Rucksack

MATERIALS
One 50g ball each of Rowan Cotton 4 ply in Light Blue (A) and Mid Blue (B). Small amounts of Light Olive (C), White (D) and Navy (E).
Pair of 3¾mm (No 9/US 5) knitting needles.

MEASUREMENTS
Rucksack is 15cm/6in wide by 15cm/6in high.

TENSION
24 sts and 33 rows to 10cm/4in over st st on 3¾mm (No 9/US 5) needles and yarn used double.

BACK AND FRONT (alike)
Stripe Sequence
6 rows A, 1 row B, 2 rows C, 3 rows B, 1 row A, 1 row E, 1 row D, 1 row A, 3 rows B, 1 row C, 1 row A, 1 row D, 1 row C, 1 row B, 1 row E, 5 rows A, 2 rows B, 1 row D, 1 row C, 2 rows A, 4 rows B, 2 rows A, 2 rows C, 1 row A, 1 row E, 1 row C, 1 row A, 2 rows B.

To Make
With 3¾mm (No 9/US 5) needles and A used double, cast on 36 sts.
Cont in st st and work first 18 rows of stripe patt using all yarns double throughout.

Shape Top
Row 1 K2, k2tog, k to last 4 sts, skpo, k2.
Row 2 P to end.
Rep the last 2 rows until 4 sts rem.
Cont in A only on these 4 sts for strap until strap measures 50cm/19½in.
Cast off.

TO MAKE UP
With right sides together, enclosing one strap end in each side seam 1cm/½in above cast-on edges, join cast-on edges and first 32 rows of side seams, turn to right side.

Zipped Jacket

MATERIALS

7(8:9) 50g balls of Rowan all seasons cotton.

Pair of 4½mm (No 7/US 7) knitting needles.

25(30:35)cm/9¾(11¾:13¾)in open-ended zip fastener.

MEASUREMENTS

To fit ages	1	2	3	years
Actual measurements				
Chest	62	70	78	cm
	24½	27½	30¾	in
Length	30	35	40	cm
	11¾	13¾	15¾	in
Sleeve length	19	22	25	cm
	7½	8¾	10	in

TENSION

18 sts and 25 rows to 10cm/4in over st st on 4½mm (No 7/US 7) needles.

BACK

With 4½mm (No 7/US 7) needles cast on 56(63:70) sts.

Beg with a k row, work in st st until Back measures 30(35:40)cm/11¾(13¾:15¾)in from cast-on edge, ending with a p row.

Shape Shoulders

Cast off 9(10:11) sts at beg of next 2 rows and 8(9:10) sts at beg of foll 2 rows.

Cast off rem 22(25:28) sts.

POCKET LININGS (make 2)

With 4½mm (No 7/US 7) needles cast on 19(21:23) sts.

Beg with a k row, work in st st for 10(11:12)cm/4(4¼:4¾)in, ending with a p row.

Leave these sts on a spare needle.

LEFT FRONT

With 4½mm (No 7/US 7) needles cast on 28(31:35) sts.

Row 1 (right side) K to end.

Row 2 K3, p to end.

Rep the last 2 rows until Front measures 12(13:14)cm/4¾(5¼:5½)in from cast-on edge, ending with a right side row.

Shape Pocket Top

Next row K3, p21(23:26) sts, turn and work on these sts.

Cast off 4 sts at beg of next row.

Dec one st at shaped edge of every row until 5(5:6) sts rem, ending with a wrong side row.

Leave these sts on a holder.

Place Pocket

With wrong side facing, rejoin yarn, p to end.

Next row K4(5:6) sts at side edge, then k across sts of Pocket

Lining. 23(26:29) sts.

Beg with a p row, work 15(17:19) rows in st st, ending with a p row.

Next row K these sts, then k5(5:6) sts from holder. 28(31:35) sts.

Cont straight until Front measures 25(30:35)cm/10(11¾:13¾)in from cast-on edge, ending with a wrong side row.

Shape Neck

Next row K to last 7(8:9) sts, leave these sts on a safety pin.

Dec one st at neck edge on every row until 17(19:21) sts rem.

Work straight until Front measures same as Back to shoulder, ending at side edge.

Shape Shoulder

Cast off 9(10:11) sts at beg of next row.

Work 1 row.

Cast off rem 8(9:10) sts.

RIGHT FRONT

With 4½mm (No 7/US 7) needles cast on 28(31:35) sts.

Row 1 (right side) K to end.

Row 2 P to last 3 sts, k3.

Rep the last 2 rows until Front measures 12(13:14)cm/4¾(5¼:5½)in from cast-on edge, ending with a wrong side row.

Shape Pocket Top

Next row K24(26:29) sts, turn and work on these sts.

Cast off 4 sts at beg of next row.

Dec one st at shaped edge of every row until 5(5:6) sts rem, ending with a right side row.

Leave these sts on a holder.

Place Pocket

Next row K across sts of Pocket Lining, then k4(5:6) sts at side edge. 23(26:29) sts.

Beg with a p row, work 16(18:20) rows in st st, ending with a k row.

Next row P these sts then p2(2:3), k3 sts from holder. 28(31:35) sts.

Cont straight until Front measures 25(30:35)cm/10(11¾:13¾)in from cast-on edge, ending with a wrong side row.

Shape Neck

Next row K7(8:9) sts, leave these sts on a safety pin, k to end.

Dec one st at neck edge on every row until 17(19:21) sts rem.

Work straight until Front measures same as Back to shoulder, ending at side edge.

Shape Shoulders

Cast off 9(10:11) sts at beg of next row.

Work 1 row.

Cast off rem 8(9:10) sts.

SLEEVES

With 4½mm (No 7/US 7) needles cast on 34(37:40) sts.

Work in st st, inc one st at each end of the 3rd and every foll 4th row until there are 54(59:64) sts.

Cont straight until Sleeve measures 19(22:25)cm/7½(8¾:10)in from cast-on edge, ending with a wrong-side row.

Cast off.

HOOD

Join shoulder seams.

With 4½mm (No 7/US 7) needles and right side facing, slip 7(8:9) sts from safety pin onto a needle, pick up and k20 sts up right side of Front neck, k 32(36:40) sts from Back neck, pick up and k20 sts down left side of Front neck, 7(8:9) sts from safety pin. 86(92:98) sts.

Work in st st with 3 sts at each end in gst for 20(21:22)cm/ 7¾ (8¼:8½)in, ending with a wrong-side row.

Shape Top

Next row Patt 43(46:49) sts, turn and work on these sts. Cast off 6 sts at beg of next and 4(4:5) foll alt rows. Work 1 row.

Cast off rem 13(16:13) sts.

Rejoin yarn to rem sts, complete to match first side.

POCKET TOPS

With 4½mm (No 7/US 7) needles and right side facing, pick up and k20(22:24) sts along shaped edge of pocket opening.

K 3 rows.

Cast off.

TO MAKE UP

Sew on Sleeves. Join side and Sleeve seams. Sew down Pocket Linings and Pocket Tops. Sew in zip, starting 1cm/½in from cast-on edge.

Rowan yarn addresses

Rowan Yarns are widely available in yarn shops. For details of stockists and mail order sources of Rowan Yarns, please write to or contact the distributors listed below.

UNITED KINGDOM
Debbie Bliss
365 St John Street
London EC1V 4LB
Tel: (020) 7833 8255
Fax: (020) 7833 3588
website: www.debbiebliss.freeserve.co.uk

Rowan Yarns
Green Lane Mill
Holmfirth
West Yorkshire HD7 1RW
Tel: (01484) 681 881

USA
Westminster Fibres
5 Northern Boulevard
Amherst
NH 03031
Tel: (603) 886 5041/5043

AUSTRALIA
Sunspun
185 Canterbury Rd
Canterbury 3126
Tel: (61) 5979 1555

BELGIUM
Pavan
Koningin Astridlaan 78
B9000 Gent
Tel: (092) 21 85 94

CANADA
Diamond Yarn
9698 St Laurent
Montreal
QUEBEC H3L 2NI
Tel: (514) 388 6188

Martin Ross
Unit 3
Toronto
Ontario M3J 2L9
Tel: (416) 736 6111

DENMARK
Ruzicka
Hydesbyvej 27
DK 4990 Saskoing
Tel: (8) 54 70 78 04

FRANCE
Elle Tricote
8 rue de Coq
67000 Strasbourg
Tel: (33) 388 23 03 13

GERMANY
Wolle + Design
Wolfshover Strasse 76
52428 Julich Stetternich
Tel: (49) 2461 54735

HOLLAND
de Afstap
Oude Leliestraat 12
1015 Amsterdam
Tel: (020) 623 1445

HONG KONG
East Unity Company Ltd
RM902
Block A
Kailey Industrial Centre
12 Fung Yip Street
Chai Wan
Tel: (852) 2869 7110

ICELAND
Stockurinn
Kjorgardi
Laugavegi 59
ICE-101 Reykjavik
Tel: (01) 551 82 58

JAPAN
Diakeito Co Ltd
2-3-11 Senba-Higashi
Minoh City
Osaka 562
Tel: (0727) 27 6604

NEW ZEALAND
Alternatives
PO Box 47 961
Auckland
Tel: (64) 9 376 0337

John Q Goldingham
PO Box 45083
Epuni
Lower Hutt
Tel: (64) 4 567 4085

NORWAY
c/o Ruzicka
(see Denmark)

SWEDEN
Vincent
Norrtulsgaten 65
11345 Stockholm
Tel: (08) 673 70 60

Yarn, kits, ready-to-wear garments, books and toys are available from Debbie Bliss's shop (see address above).
Contact shop for information regarding workshops.

Acknowledgements

This book would not have been possible without the invaluable help of the following:

Most important, the dedicated band of knitters: Pat Church, Connie Critchell, Jacqui Dunt, Janet Fagan, Penny Hill, Shirley Kennet, Maisie Lawrence, Beryl Salter and Frances Wallace.

Jane Bunce and Jane Crowfoot who contributed the Striped Rucksack and Alpaca Bolero.

Tina Egleton, for Nellie the sheep.

The children – a big thank you to: Sam and Max, Robert, Thea, Scarlet, Poppy, Conner, Olive and Ben.

Marilyn Wilson and Penny Hill who checked the patterns.

Sandra Lane, who created beautiful pictures, and made even the still-lives look delicious.

Sammi Bell, the inspirational stylist; who made many of the accessories to coordinate perfectly with the knits.

Heather Jeeves, the perfect agent.

Denise Bates, whose patience never fails to amaze me, and who is a great support throughout each project.

Emma Callery, for her thoughtful and precise editing of the book.

Ciara Lunn, the editorial assistant, who combines the perfect mix of efficiency with a great sense of humour.

Christine Wood, for her fresh approach to *Baby Style*'s look.